# DUNE COMPANION

## Novels Reading Order, Characters, Planets and More in Frank Herbert's Books Series

**Ted West**

# CONTENTS

# Foreword

**Have you been searching for the best Dune reading order? Or maybe more information about the Dune universe?**

We've got some good news for you; your search ends here.

The forthcoming remake of Dune by Denis Villeneuve has led to renewed interest in the 1965 expansive sci-fi classic from Frank Herbert and the immense realm it birthed. Nevertheless, getting the right sequence for the books can be quite onerous.

The labyrinthine nature of Dune novels is a well-known fact; it boasts sprawling plots, bizarre character names, and some enchanting themes.

Despite the above, anyone who has followed Dune in the right order will attest that the series ranks amongst the best sci-fi novels of all time.

This guide will show you how to read the Dune books by Frank Herbert in order while showing you other novels written by his son Brian and sci-fi author, Kevin J. Anderson. The guide will also help you navigate the Dune books and better understand the meaning of the novels.

**Since this book includes:**

-- Reading order of dune books;

-- Description of the main characters of the books;

-- Links to all the books of dune;

-- Description of the planets;

-- Themes and ideas in the dune novels.

## Thank You for Purchasing & Reading!

**I hope you find the information useful and easy to use.**

# WHAT IS DUNE?

Ted West

Dune refers to the science fiction media franchise, which emerged with Frank Herbert's 1965 novel and continued afterward to publish other works of fiction up to 2020. Dune has been referred to as the best-selling science fiction novel ever written. It won the 1966 Hugo Award and the inaugural Nebula Award for Best Novel. It was adapted into a movie in 1984 and a television miniseries in 2000. There were five sequels to the original text, all written by the author, two of which were also made into a miniseries in 2003.

The world of the text has become the major inspiration for several real-world endeavors, and a major application is the creation of conventional games and popular video games that mirror the Dune universe. The names of planets from the Dune novel have also been used since 2009 for real plains and other features on Saturn's moon, Titan.

After Frank Herbert's Demise in 1986, his son Brian Herbert and Science Fiction author Kevin J. Anderson published a few prequels, beginning from 1999. They also published two books that ensured the resolution of the original Dune series, Hunters of Dune, published in 2006, and the Sandworms of Dune, released in 2007, both of which were partly informed by Frank Herbert's notes found ten years after the author's demise.

The Dune universe or 'Duniverse' refers to the world of the Dune text, which includes the political, scientific, and social setting. The Dune saga is set tens of thousands of years in the future and tells of a civilization with advanced technology and physical abilities despite forbidding computers or "thinking machines" of all kinds. The harsh desert planet of Arrakis, the only known source of the spice, Melange, is extremely important to the Dune Empire.

Critics have pointed out a Middle Eastern influence in Herbert's writing numerous times. This is because of parallels discovered between some of Herbert's words and ideas and concepts found in the Arabic language and the series "Islamic undertones."

# GETTING TO GRIPS WITH THE WORLD OF DUNE

The universe of Dune is set in a fictional, futuristic world, specifically, the year 10,191, where great houses govern feudal societies with their dominion spanning several planets called fiefs. Fief in this context refers to estates held by individuals who owe allegiance to a higher authority.

Duke Leto Atreides and a Bene Gesserit acolyte known as Lady Jessica were the parents of the protagonist, Paul Atreides. His mother's sect, Bene Gesserit, is a matriarchal religious group possessing evident superhuman abilities achieved after long years of tasking physical and mental exercises. The Bene Gesserit are driven by their own political motives and are often in pursuit of more power, which played a great part in the installation of Lady Jessica in the Atreides house.

The Bene Gesserit are distrusted by most of the people who refer to them as 'witches' due to their extraordinary abilities. To birth a male child, the Bene Gesserit acolytes eventually have to partake in an institutionalized breeding program. The male child birthed through this process is a Christ-like figure, referred to as the Kwisatz Haderach.

The novel opens with the Atreides family moving from the ocean planet Caladan to Arrakis to manage the harvest of an essential export referred to as Melange, called spice in the local parlance of the desert planet of Arrakis. Duke Leto goes on this expedition under the orders of the Padishah Emperor Shaddam IV, who is secretly working with House Horkennen, known enemies of House Atreides. Danger will come quickly to the Atreides, forcing Jessica and Paul to seek safety amongst the Fremen, Arrakis' aboriginal people who dwell in the hazardous sand dunes.

# DEVELOPMENT AND PUBLICATION

## *Original Series*

Herbert's choice of setting is said to have been a result of research he started in 1957 – for an article which was never written – concerning the Department of Agriculture in the United States, who were conducting an experiment aimed at stabilizing damaging sand dunes with the aid of poverty grasses. These sand dunes could "swallow whole cities, lakes, rivers, and highways." Herbert would spend the succeeding five years in researching, writing, and revising what would turn out to be the novel Dune, published originally as a series in the Analog Magazine as two shorter works: Dune World (1963) and the prophet of Dune (1965).

This initial version would later be expanded, reworked – rejected by over 20 publishers – before Chilton Books, a publishing house that gained acclaim for their auto repair manual,s published the text in 1965. Dune will go on to take home the 1966 Hugo Award and the inaugural Nebula Award for Best Novel. It has sold close to 20 million copies and is available in dozens of languages. Dune is recognized amongst the bestselling sci-fi novels of all time.

In 1969, a sequel to Dune was published with the title, "Dune Messiah," while a third installment, "Children of Dune," which eventually received a Hugo Award nomination, was published in 1976. Children of Dune would make history as the first hardcover best-seller in the sci-fi sub-genre. Herbert had written parts of both sequels even before he completed Dune.

In 1978, Berkeley Books published an illustrated version of Dune, which had 33 black-and-white sketches and eight full-color paintings made by John Schoenherr, the same artist who had handled the cover art for the first Dune publication and illustrated the Dune and Children of Dune series on Analog Magazine. In 1980, Herbert revealed his surprise when he discovered that the artwork by Schoenherr, including the sandworms, Baron Harkomena, and the Sardaukar, mirrored his own imagination, even though he had not spoken to the artist before he created the paintings.

When Herbert published "God Emperor of Dune" in 1981, Publishers Weekly ranked it the #11 hardcover fiction best-seller of 1981. Heretics of Dune hit the markets in 1984 and ranked #13 on the hardcover fiction best-seller; this would be followed quickly by Chapterhouse: Dune in 1985. Herbert passed away on February 11, 1986.

## Brian Herbert And Kevin J. Anderson

More than ten years after Herbert's demise, his son Brian teamed up with Kevin J. Anderson, the science fiction author, to coauthor a trilogy of Dune prequels, later referred to as the Prelude to Dune series.

They made use of Frank Herbert's personal notes in creating "Dune: House Atreides in 1999, Dune: House Harkonnen in 2000, and Dune: House Corrino in 2001, all of which had their setting as the years before the main events of Dune. Another trilogy of Dune prequels, referred to as "The Legends of Dune," would follow the first and contain such texts as "Dune: The Butlerian Jihad in 2002,

Dune: The Machine Crusade in 2003, and "Dune: The Battle of Corrin in 2004.

This was set 10,000 years before the main events in Dune and was made possible by a particular back story element created by Herbert himself, which he referred to as the Butlerian Jihad. It was a short description of humanity's "Crusade against computers, thinking machines, and conscious robots" and was now made more elaborate by Brian and Anderson in this second trilogy.

After he'd drawn up an outline and a proposal for the first book of the Prelude to Dune trilogy and sent both off to the publisher, Brian happened upon his father's 30-page draft for a sequel to the ChapterHouse Dune, which Frank Herbert had tagged Dune 7. After six publications, Brian Herbert and Anderson would publish Hunters of Dune in 2006 and Sandworms of Dune in 2007. The last two publications were written to bring the original Frank Herbert writings to a conclusion.

The Heroes of Dune series, set in the time between Herbert's original novels, arrived next. The first two were "Paul of Dune" in 2008 and "The Winds of Dune," published in 2009. The publication of another two, called "The Throne of Dune and Leto of Dune (Likely to become "The Golden Path of Dune") was postponed because of proposals to publish a trilogy about "The formation of the Bene Gesserit, the mentats, the Suk Doctors, the spacing guild and the navigators, as well as solidifying "The Corrino Imperium." In 2012, "Sisterhood of Dune" was published while "Mentas of Dune" followed in 2014. In a 2009 interview, Anderson opined that the third and final would be called "The Swordmasters of Dune," but it was renamed "Navigators of Dune" in 2014 and went into the market in 2016.

Herbert and Anderson announced another prequel trilogy named the "Caladan Trilogy" in July 2020. The first book in the series, "The Duke of Caladan," is billed for publication in October 2020.

In 2013, John Michaud of the New Yorker wrote, "The conversion of Dune into a franchise, while pleasing readers and earning royalties for the Herbert estate, has gone a long way towards obscuring the power of the original novel."

# Dune Short Stories

1985 was the year Frank Herbert penned "The Road to Dune." It is an illustrated short work whose timeframe setting is sometime between the Dune events and Dune Messiah. It is among 12 other short fiction stories that made up the anthology titled Eye by Frank Herbert. The story is a guidebook that takes tourists on pilgrims to Arrakis. In the book, you'll find images with descriptions that talk about some of the devices and characters in the Dune novels.

Several Dune short stories have also been penned by Brian Herbert and Anderson. As you go through these short stories, you would realize that they are related to the novels by Frank Herbert and that there isn't much diversion from the Dune novels. These short stories include, in chronological order, "Dune: A Whisper of Caladan Seas" in 2001, "Dune: Hunting Harkonnens" in 2002, "Dune: Whipping Mek" in 2003, "Dune: The Faces of a Martyr" in 2004, "Dune: Sea Child" in 2006, and "Dune: Treasure in the Sand" also in 2006.

# WHERE DO I START READING THE DUNE STORIES?

Ted West

Most stories with a long series have one thing in common: disagreement is always stirred amongst fans about where to begin to enjoy the series from. Apparently, it is the same with the Dune series. While some fans claim that it is better to start the Dune fictional journey in chronological order (see the list below), others believe that the best option is to read them according to how they were published. I have a different opinion; you should begin the series from the story that shone the spotlight on the entire Dune series; that is the first installment in the Dune series: Dune.

In other words, start the Dune Saga from the original series by Frank Herbert himself. Although the original Dune saga comprises six novels, I tend to think of it as a three-book saga and a three-book sequel. Of course, this Dune division is not without reason. After the third installment in the Dune saga, Children of Dune was published, and the fourth installment, God Emperor of Dune, was published after a few centuries had gone by. The centuries gap between the publication of the third and fourth novel accounts for my inability to view the books as being on the same level.

**Keep reading to discover the original Dune saga books according to how they were published as well as some details on them:**

➢ Dune
➢ Dune Messiah
➢ Children of Dune

If you have decided not to read any more Dune sagas, ensure you read the above highlighted first three installments in the Dune franchise. In them, you will discover how Paul Atreides' story ends. Obviously, Dune is still alive after Paul's demise, and if you read these three books you will know how the story of Paul Atreides concludes. Of course, Dune keeps living after him.

After reading the first three installments, if you crave more Dune, which is inevitable, you have more Dune at your disposal.

**Here is the three-book sequel:**

➢ God Emperor of Dune
➢ Heretics of Dune
➢ Chapterhouse: Dune

Sadly, the last installments, Chapterhouse: Dune ends with a spine-chiller. Most of the plotlines were not resolved because of the author's demise the following year after the book was published in 1985.

**Nevertheless, Brian Herbert and Kevin Anderson resolved the hanging plotlines by writing the next two Dune novels titled:**

- ➤ Hunters of Dune
- ➤ Sandworms of Dune

The Dune reading order becomes complicated from these two Dune novels by Brian and Kevin. Note: Frank Herbert didn't pen the prequels and sequels that you are about to see. As seen above, Frank Herbert only penned the first six Dune novels as discussed above.

In the story's timeline, the first prequel comes before the first Dune book by Frank Herbert. Hence, the incidents in the first prequel occurred before the Arrakis conflict broke loose. It appears that the prequel is told from the point of view of three Nobel houses.

**The manuscript is named after the noble houses:**

- ➤ House Atreides
- ➤ House Harkonnen
- ➤ House Corrino

The following is the second prequel that tells the story that happened many thousand years before the first novel in the original Dune series. They are:

- ➤ The Butlerian Jihad
- ➤ The Machine Crusade
- ➤ The Battle of Corrin

**Then, here's the sequel trilogy of the second prequel trilogy:**

- ➤ Sisterhood of Dune

- ➢ Mentats of Dune
- ➢ Navigators of Dune

In July 2020, Brian Herbert and Kevin revealed that a new prequel trilogy would be released called the Caladan Trilogy. Once released, we will know which order it falls in.

Aside from these highlighted prequels and sequels, there are tons of Dune short stories. In the "Dune's Chronology: the reading order" section, we expose more about the Duniverse.

# DUNE'S CHRONOLOGY: THE READING ORDER

If you want to follow the chronological reading order of the Duniverse, including the short stories, keep reading.

## 1. Hunting Harkonnens

Type: Short Story. Released: 2002. Author: Brian Herbert, Kevin J. Anderson.

## 2. The Butlerian Jihad

It is the first book in the Legends of Dune prequel trilogy, which takes place over 10,000 years before the events of Frank Herbert's celebrated 1965 novel Dune. The series chronicles the fictional Butlerian Jihad, a crusade by the last free humans in the universe against the thinking machines, a violent and dominating force led by the sentient computer Omnius.

Dune: The Butlerian Jihad rose to #7 on The New York Times Best Seller list in its second week of publication.

Type: Novel. Released: 2002. Author: Brian Herbert, Kevin J. Anderson.

## 3. *Whipping Mek*

Type: Short Story. Released: 2003. Author: Brian Herbert, Kevin J. Anderson.

## 4. *The Machine Crusade*

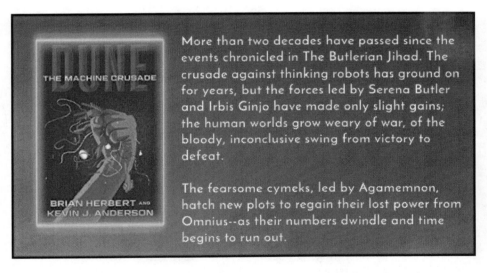

More than two decades have passed since the events chronicled in The Butlerian Jihad. The crusade against thinking robots has ground on for years, but the forces led by Serena Butler and Irbis Ginjo have made only slight gains; the human worlds grow weary of war, of the bloody, inconclusive swing from victory to defeat.

The fearsome cymeks, led by Agamemnon, hatch new plots to regain their lost power from Omnius--as their numbers dwindle and time begins to run out.

Type: Novel. Released: 2003. Author: Brian Herbert, Kevin J. Anderson.

## 5. *The Faces of a Martyr*

Type: Short Story. Released: 2004. Author: Brian Herbert, Kevin J.

Anderson.

# 6. The Battle of Corrin

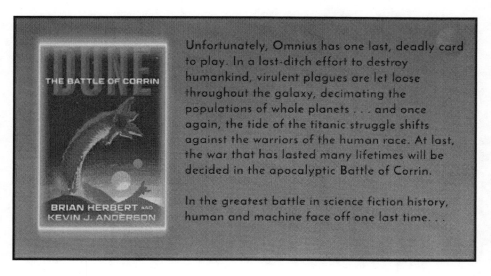

Unfortunately, Omnius has one last, deadly card to play. In a last-ditch effort to destroy humankind, virulent plagues are let loose throughout the galaxy, decimating the populations of whole planets . . . and once again, the tide of the titanic struggle shifts against the warriors of the human race. At last, the war that has lasted many lifetimes will be decided in the apocalyptic Battle of Corrin.

In the greatest battle in science fiction history, human and machine face off one last time. . .

Type: Novel. Released: 2004. Author: Brian Herbert, Kevin J. Anderson.

# 7. Sisterhood of Dune

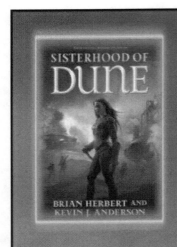

It is eighty-three years after the last of the thinking machines were destroyed in the Battle of Corrin, after Faykan Butler took the name of Corrino and established himself as the first Emperor of a new Imperium. Great changes are brewing that will shape and twist all of humankind.

The war hero Vorian Atreides has turned his back on politics and Salusa Secundus. The descendants of Abulurd Harkonnen Griffen and Valya have sworn vengeance against Vor, blaming him for the downfall of their fortunes.

Type: Novel. Released: 2012. Author: Brian Herbert, Kevin J. Anderson.

# 8. Mentats of Dune

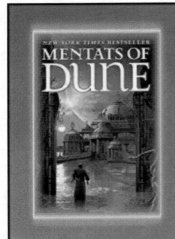

In Brian Herbert and Kevin J. Anderson's Mentats of Dune, the thinking machines have been defeated but the struggle for humanity's future continues.

The Mentats, the Navigators, and the Sisterhood all strive to improve the human race, but each group knows that as Butlerian fanaticism grows stronger, the battle will be to choose the path of humanity's future—whether to embrace civilization, or to plunge into an endless dark age.

Type: Novel. Released: 2014. Author: Brian Herbert, Kevin J. Anderson.

# 9. Red Plague

Type: Short Story. Released: 2016. Author: Brian Herbert, Kevin J. Anderson.

# 10. Navigators of Dune

Brian Herbert and Kevin J. Anderson's Navigators of Dune is the climactic finale of the Great Schools of Dune trilogy, set 10,000 years before Frank Herbert's classic Dune.

The story line tells the origins of the Bene Gesserit Sisterhood and its breeding program, the human-computer Mentats, and the Navigators (the Spacing Guild), as well as a crucial battle for the future of the human race, in which reason faces off against fanaticism. These events have far-reaching consequences that will set the stage for Dune, millennia later.

Type: Novel. Released: 2016. Author: Brian Herbert, Kevin J. Anderson.

# 11. House Atreides

The tale of Pardot Kynes, ambitious planetologist dispatched to the sands of Arrakis to understand the origins of the spice melange, the most valuable substance in the known universe.

And the tale of Crown Prince Shaddam Corrino, whose lust for power leads him to plot the assassination of his own father and to create a plan that will replace the spice and disrupt the Imperium forever . . .

Type: Novel. Released: 1999. Author: Brian Herbert, Kevin J. Anderson.

# 12. House Harkonnen

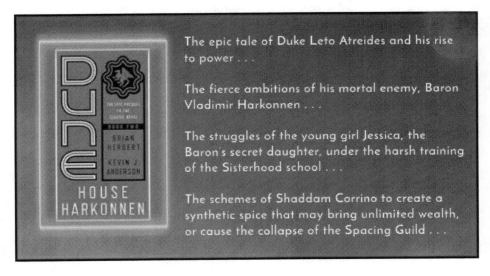

The epic tale of Duke Leto Atreides and his rise to power . . .

The fierce ambitions of his mortal enemy, Baron Vladimir Harkonnen . . .

The struggles of the young girl Jessica, the Baron's secret daughter, under the harsh training of the Sisterhood school . . .

The schemes of Shaddam Corrino to create a synthetic spice that may bring unlimited wealth, or cause the collapse of the Spacing Guild . . .

Type: Novel. Released: 2000. Author: Brian Herbert, Kevin J. Anderson.

# 13. House Corrino

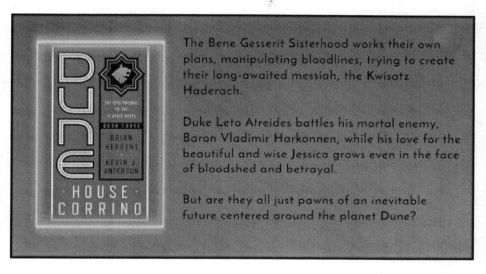

Type: Novel. Released: 2001. Author: Brian Herbert, Kevin J. Anderson.

# 14. Wedding Silk

Type: Short Story. Released: 2011. Author: Brian Herbert, Kevin J. Anderson.

# 15. Paul of Dune (Parts II, IV, VI)

PAUL OF DUNE begins the story of those twelve fateful years and the wars of the jihad of Paul Muad'Dib.

It is an epic of battle and betrayal; of love and idealism; of ambition and intrigue. Above all, it is the story of how Paul Atreides - who achieved absolute power when scarcely more than a boy - changes from an idealist into a dictator who is the prisoner of the bureaucrats and fanatics who surround him.

Type: Novel. Released: 2008. Author: Brian Herbert, Kevin J. Anderson.

# 16. The Winds of Dune (Part II, excluding Interlude)

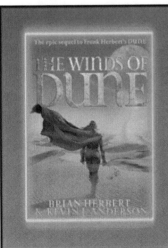

Paul Atreides is the man who overthrew a corrupt empire and then launched a terrible jihad across the galaxy, shedding the blood of trillions. The now-hated tyrant, the blind emperor Paul Muad'Dib, has walked off into the endless desert of the planet Arrakis, known as Dune, leaving his turbulent empire without guidance.

It's up to his mother Jessica, with her daughter Alia, the brave troubadour-warrior Gurney Halleck, the Fremen leader Stilgar, as well as Paul's wife-in-name and biographer, Princess Irulan, to try and hold an empire together even as it tears itself apart from within and without.

Type: Novel. Released: 2009. Author: Brian Herbert, Kevin J. Anderson.

# 17. Dune

Frank Herbert's classic masterpiece—a triumph of the imagination and one of the bestselling science fiction novels of all time.

Set on the desert planet Arrakis, Dune is the story of the boy Paul Atreides, heir to a noble family tasked with ruling an inhospitable world where the only thing of value is the "spice" melange, a drug capable of extending life and enhancing consciousness. Coveted across the known universe, melange is a prize worth killing for....

Type: Novel. Released: 1965. Author: Frank Herbert.

# 18. Whisper of Caladan Seas

Type: Short Story. Released: 2009. Author: Brian Herbert, Kevin J. Anderson.

# 19. The Waters of Kanly

Type: Short Story. Released: 2017. Author: Brian Herbert, Kevin J. Anderson.

## 20. Paul of Dune (Parts I, III, V, VII)

Type: Novel. Released: 2008. Author: Brian Herbert, Kevin J. Anderson.

## 21. The Winds of Dune (Part IV, excluding Interlude)

Type: Novel. Released: 2009. Author: Brian Herbert, Kevin J. Anderson.

## 22. The Road to Dune

Type: Short Story. Released: 1985. Author: Frank Herbert.

## 23. Dune Messiah

Dune Messiah continues the story of Paul Atreides, better known—and feared—as the man christened Muad'Dib. As Emperor of the known universe, he possesses more power than a single man was ever meant to wield. Worshipped as a religious icon by the fanatical Fremen, Paul faces the enmity of the political houses he displaced when he assumed the throne.

And even as House Atreides begins to crumble around him from the machinations of his enemies, the true threat to Paul comes to his lover, Chani, and the unborn heir to his family's dynasty...

Type: Novel. Released: 1969. Author: Frank Herbert.

# 24. The Winds of Dune (Parts I, II: Interlude, III, IV: Interlude, V)

Type: Novel. Released: 2009. Author: Brian Herbert, Kevin J. Anderson.

# 25. Children of Dune

The Children of Dune are twin siblings Leto and Ghanima Atreides, whose father, the Emperor Paul Muad'Dib, disappeared in the desert wastelands of Arrakis nine years ago.

Like their father, the twins possess supernormal abilities—making them valuable to their manipulative aunt Alia, who rules the Empire in the name of House Atreides...

Type: Novel. Released: 1976. Author: Frank Herbert.

# 26. God Emperor of Dune

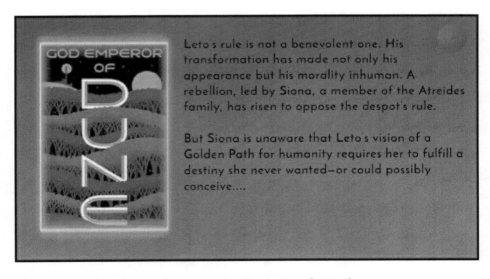

Leto's rule is not a benevolent one. His transformation has made not only his appearance but his morality inhuman. A rebellion, led by Siona, a member of the Atreides family, has risen to oppose the despot's rule.

But Siona is unaware that Leto's vision of a Golden Path for humanity requires her to fulfill a destiny she never wanted—or could possibly conceive....

Type: Novel. Released: 1981. Author: Frank Herbert.

# 27. Heretics of Dune

Now the Lost Ones are returning home in pursuit of power. And as these factions vie for control over the remnants of the Empire, a girl named Sheeana rises to prominence in the wastelands of Rakis, sending religious fervor throughout the galaxy.

For she possesses the abilities of the Fremen sandriders—fulfilling a prophecy foretold by the late God Emperor....

Type: Novel. Released: 1984. Author: Frank Herbert.

# 28. Chapterhouse: Dune

Under the leadership of Mother Superior Darwi Odrade, the Bene Gesserit have colonized a green world on the planet Chapterhouse and are turning it into a desert, mile by scorched mile. And once they've mastered breeding sandworms, the Sisterhood will control the production of the greatest commodity in the known galaxy—the spice melange.

But their true weapon remains a man who has lived countless lifetimes—a man who served under the God Emperor Paul Muad'Dib....

Type: Novel. Released: 1985. Author: Frank Herbert.

# 29. Sea Child

Type: Short Story. Released: 2006. Author: Brian Herbert, Kevin J. Anderson.

# 30. Hunters of Dune

Hunters of Dune and the concluding volume, Sandworms of Dune, bring together the great story lines and beloved characters in Frank Herbert's classic Dune universe, ranging from the time of the Butlerian Jihad to the original Dune series and beyond.

Based directly on Frank Herbert's final outline, which lay hidden in a safe-deposit box for a decade, these two volumes will finally answer the urgent questions Dune fans have been debating for two decades.

Type: Novel. Released: 2006. Author: Brian Herbert, Kevin J. Anderson.

# 31. Treasure in the Sand

Type: Short Story. Released: 2006. Author: Brian Herbert, Kevin J. Anderson.

# 32. Sandworms of Dune

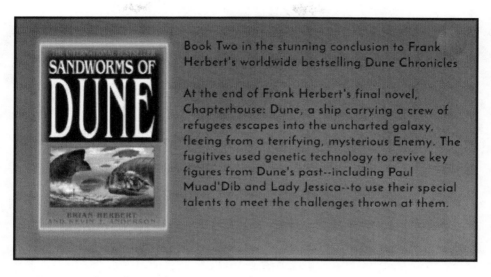

Book Two in the stunning conclusion to Frank Herbert's worldwide bestselling Dune Chronicles

At the end of Frank Herbert's final novel, Chapterhouse: Dune, a ship carrying a crew of refugees escapes into the uncharted galaxy, fleeing from a terrifying, mysterious Enemy. The fugitives used genetic technology to revive key figures from Dune's past--including Paul Muad'Dib and Lady Jessica--to use their special talents to meet the challenges thrown at them.

Type: Novel. Released: 2007. Author: Brian Herbert, Kevin J. Anderson.

# HOUSES

Major Houses are the Houses in the Empire, holding entire planets as fiefdoms.

## 1. House Atreides

## Origin

In ancient times, the Greek noble family Atreides, descended from the legendary Atreus, took a prominent position during the Butlerian Jihad.

## Location

Up until the Duke of Leto I, House Atreides was based and ruled on the planet Caladan. It was a fief granted to the House by the Emperor. The Atreides have ruled the planet for 26 generations. A competent economic, social, and foreign policy led to the prosperity of this beautiful world and the emergence of a civilized, contented, well-organized, spiritual society.

Although Caladan had a fairly low level of industrial development, the Atreides tried to preserve the pristine purity and beauty of this planet. It is known that mentats, masters of the sword, masters of battle, excellent scientists and strategists trained on the planet. The Atreides also had a developed army. All soldiers were taught a special military language of the Atreides, which consisted of imperceptible finger gestures, facial expressions, etc.

# 2. House Harkonnen

House Harkonnen is one of the Great Houses of the intergalactic feudal empire. Representatives of House Harkonnen play a significant role in the Dune Universe. According to the book "Dune: House Harkonnen," the Harkonnen coat of arms is a blue griffin, but in the" Encyclopedia of Dune," the head of a ram is indicated as the coat of arms, and in the video game Emperor: Battle for Dune — the head of a tour.

## Characteristic Features

The Harkonnens are the main opponents of the Atreides genus and are described as their antipodes. Their enmity began with the friction between the progenitors of their families. While the Atreides are described as noble people of honor, the Harkonnen appear to be ambitious, not averse to meanness and intrigue.

The generic name Harkonnen comes from the Finnish name Härkönen. The very name Härkönen, in turn, was formed from the Finnish word härkä-ox.

# 3. House Corrino

House Corrino is one of the Great Houses, the ruling family of the galactic feudal empire in the Known Universe.

House Corrino came to power after the victory of mankind over the thinking machines in the battle for Corrin (after which they took their name). Representatives of House Corrino ruled for about 10,000 years until they were overthrown by Muad'Dib.

## Famous Representatives

1. Idriss Corrino I

2. Shaddam Corrino IV

3. Irulan Corrino

4. Wensicia Corrino

5. Farad'n Corrino

## Additionally

Dune: House Corrino is a novel by Brian Herbert and Kevin Anderson, which takes place in the universe created by Frank Herbert (published in 2001).

# 4. House Ginaz

House Ginaz is a proud and honest family with little storyline in the Dune Universe, created by writer Frank Herbert. House Ginaz is one of the Great Houses of the intergalactic feudal empire, which appeared during the reign of the second generation of House Corrino - the imperial family of Hassik Corrino III. Duncan Idaho - House Ginaz's weaponsmith, is one of the key characters in the Dune Universe, appearing in every book by Frank Herbert.

## Characteristic Features

House Ginaz are allies of House Atreides and mortal enemies of House Moritani. Frank Herbert himself mentions in his reference book to Dune that House Ginaz is an ally of House Atreides. The Encyclopedia of Dune gives more specific information: Camillo III Ginaz concluded in 9588 AD. A secret agreement with House Atreides, which coordinated the actions of the two Great Houses and guaranteed them support from each other in difficult times.

Ginaz had its own school of gunsmiths (sword masters). The master's training course is 8 years. And it can be passed by a representative of any great house who has paid for training. Despite the long course of study, Duncan Idaho said that Gurney Halleck, who did not study there, wins him 6 times out of 10.

# 5. House Vernius

House Vernius is a relatively young Great House, which was only a few centuries old by the time Leto I became a duke in the time of Faufreluches.

House Vernius specialized in innovative technologies. After an intensified economic war with the House of Richese, they got the right to produce heighliners for the Space Guild.

## The Reign Of Count Dominic Vernius

As a young man, Dominic Vernius provided Ixixian forces to the Padishah Emperor Elrood Corrino IX. At the same time, he met and became friends with Duke Paul I Atreides (10089 PG - 10156

PG). For his faithful service, the Padishah-emperor rewarded Dominic Vernius by expanding his flax, which became several planets under the control of House Vernius.

After the war, Dominic Vernius obtained his former concubine Lady Shando from the Padishah Emperor Elrood IX, whom he'd previously granted freedom, not knowing that she was secretly meeting with Dominic Vernius. Subsequently, Dominic Vernius married Lady Shando, thereby provoking the anger of the Padishah Emperor Elrud IX, as he was afraid that his former concubine would tell about all the secrets of the Padishah emperor's intimate life. Dominic Vernius and his wife Lady Shando had two children-Rhombur and Kailea Vernius.

# 6. House Thorvald

House Thorvald was the Great House of Landsraad during the later Corrino Empire and was located on the planet Ipyr.

## Rebelling Against Paul

During the Ascension of House Atreides a few years later, Memnon assumed the dangerous position of leader of the rebellion against the new Emperor Paul Muad'Dib. When Paul made his first speech to the Landsraad in 10194 AG after the overthrow of the Kaitain government by Jihad, Memnon walked away, shouting at Paul, "Enough of the emperors!"

Soon after, Memnon gathered the Houses that rebelled against Paul under the leadership of House Thorvald. A few years later, they organized a guarded defense of Galicia against the troops of Gurney Halleck in 10196 AG, although the Emperor's forces eventually won. After the first attempt on Paul's life in 10198 at the

Great Surrender Ceremony on Arrakis, House Thorvald initially claimed to have organized an elaborate plot, although it turned out that the organizer was Whitmore Bludd.

## Destruction Of House Thorvald

Later that year, Paul discovered through foresight that Memnon and his allies were planning to attack and destroy Caladan, as well as kidnap or kill Paul's mother, Jessica. Paul immediately summoned a representative of the Olar guild, who took him to the Beric guild navigator. It was confirmed that House Thorvald had indeed conspired to destroy Paul's homeworld and that the starfighters were on heighliners, waiting to be transported to the waterworld.

Paul ordered that all House Thorvald ships, as well as all Thorvald allies, be sent by navigator into deep space without any supplies. He further ordered the destruction of House Thorvald and the sterilization of their homeworld Ipyr, and House Thorvald ceased to exist.

# MAIN CHARACTERS

A list of the main Dune characters that most often appear in the series. To make it easier for you to navigate the novels.

## House Atreides

### *Leto Atreides*

Leto Atreides — Duke of House Atreides, father of Paul Atreides and Alia Atreides. The cousin of House Corrino on the female line, often referred to as the Red Duke. The Emperor's father is Paul Atreides.

## Biography

House Atreides ruled the family estate on Caladan with the rank of Siridar (a Galach term for "planetary") for twenty generations before being supplanted on Arrakis.

In 10191 PG, he received the planet Arrakis, the only place in the universe for the extraction of Spices, from the Padishah Emperor Shaddam IV. At the same time, the duke refused to negotiate with the head of House Harkonnen, Baron Vladimir and declared on him kanly (officially declared war of childbirth in accordance with the laws of the Great Convention and waged in accordance with their strict limitations of methods and means).

Having moved to Arrakis, Duke Leto tried to reorganize the production of Spice on the planet and prepare for the expected attack by House Harkonnen but was not ready for such a large-scale invasion.

Leto died as a result of the betrayal of Dr. Suk Wellington Yueh, who was directed by Baron Harkonnen through threats and blackmail. In order to get even with the Baron, Yueh inserted a tooth containing a strong aerosol poison into the Duke. Facing his sworn enemy, Leto tried unsuccessfully to poison Vladimir Harkonnen, but he himself died from the sprayed poison.

The remains of Duke Leto rest in the Skull Tomb on Arrakis.

Leto's son Paul named his son after him - Leto II Atreides.

# *Paul Atreides*

*«He was a warrior and a mystic, a monster and a saint, a fox and the very incarnate innocence, less than god, but more than man. You can't measure Muad'Dib with an ordinary yardstick. In the moment of his glory, he saw the death prepared for him, but he accepted the danger and met treason with his face. You will say that he did it out of a sense of justice. Good. But - whose justice? Do not forget: we are now talking about Muad'Dib, about the same Muad'Dib who ordered the war drums to be covered with the enemy's skin. About Muad'Dib, who, with a simple wave of his hand, brushed aside everything connected with his ducal past, from all customs, laws and conventions, saying only: «I am Kwisatz Haderach, and this reason is enough».»*
*— **Princess Irulan**.*

Paul Atreides, also known as Muad'Dib - Duke of House Atreides, Emperor of the Atreides Empire, The Preacher. Father of Leto II and Ghanima Atreides, husband of Princess Irulan Corrino.

## Biography

Paul was born on the ancestral planet of Atreides Caladan. His father was the Duke Leto Atreides, and his mother was the duke's concubine, the pupil of Bene Gesserit Lady Jessica.

Upon arrival at Arrakis, he was perceived by the local population, the Fremen, as the messiah (Lisan al Gaib and Mahdi). In the Sietch Tabr, he adopted the names Usul and was known among the Fremen as Muad'Dib. Under his command, the Fremen won the war for the planet Arrakis, defeating Harkonnen and the padishah-emperor Shaddam IV.

After these events, Paul married the daughter of the Padishah emperor, Princess Irulan, and became the emperor of the known Universe, but his concubine, Chani, gave birth to his children.

He lost his eyes as a result of using Stoneburner; however, as a Kwisatz Haderach, he could see what was happening in the present, past and probable future.

After the birth of the children, Leto II and Ghanima, and the death of Chani, Paul went into the desert and was considered dead but later returned in the guise of the blind The Preacher. He was killed by the priests of his sister Alia during a speech criticizing the cult of his personality and the religion of Alia.

## Appearance

He has his father's hair, black as a raven's wing, aquiline profile, oval face, straight-looking green eyes-the legacy of the Old Duke, his paternal grandfather.

# Leto Atreides II

Leto Atreides II is the second son of Muad'Dib and his concubine Chani. The God-emperor who ruled the known universe for more than three thousand years.

*"The universe is changeable, but the strangest manifestation of this variability is us, people. We respond, as resonators, to many influences . Our future needs constant adjustment. But there is a barrier that we must tear down, and this will require cruelty, we will have to rebel against our dearest, most intimate desires..."*

## Character Description

Born in 10205 PG.

As a result of the influence of Spice and genetic abnormalities transmitted to Leto II by his parents, he already had a sense of self-awareness and the life-memory of all his ancestors in the womb.

The essence of Leto II in his youth was merged with the essence of his distant ancestor who lived on Earth — Harum. Leto II could also communicate with the entities of any of his ancestors. From his father, he took over the gift of mentally "being" in many places at the same time and seeing the past, present and future as a single process.

As a result of the prophetic gift, Leto saw "The Golden Path" - the life of humanity as a single whole and sacrificed himself for the sake of the existence of people in the future. Managing a key resource of the empire - spice, he ruled like a tyrant, trying to implement the only plan he knew to preserve The Golden Path.

During his reign, he conducted his own crossbreeding program based on the descendants of Ghanima Atreides, his sister, and Farad'n Corrino. As a result, he was able to deduce the type of people who could not be seen in the streams of time. The first representative of the genus, whose future Leto could not see was Siona Atreides.

By controlling his metabolism, he entered into symbiosis with the sandtrout - a kind of protozoan living in the sand of Dune. "Trout" covered his skin and later led to the mutation of the entire body. Leto's new look made him virtually invulnerable to any type of weapon, but over 3,500 years, Leto slowly transformed into a giant sandworm. After 3500 years from the human, he only had a face, refined arms and legs-fins, the rest of the body looked like a worm.

Only death prevented the final metamorphosis: in the year 13728 PG as a result of an attempt on his life organized by Siona Atreides and the ghola Duncan Idaho. Leto's cause of death was the water of the river into which he fell from a collapsed bridge. After entering the water, the sand trout, which made up most of Leto's body, began to leave him and absorb the water. After several thousand years, this sand trout, having significantly multiplied and absorbed water from the entire planet Rakis (thereby turning it into a desert again), transformed into giant sandworms. These worms were distinguished by increased intelligence, and Bene Gesserit feared the awakening of Leto II's mind in one of them.

# Additionally

- The character appears in the book "Dune Messiah" as a new-born infant. In Children of Dune, Leto appears as an 8-year-old child; however, thanks to the memory of his ancestors, he is intellectually older than everyone around him.

- Leto's twin is his sister, Ghanima.

- He received his name in honor of his paternal grandfather Leto Atreides.

- Leto was engaged to Hwi Noree.

- He organized the Fish Speakers religion around himself.

- The conspirators and opponents of the Leto II government called him a Worm for his external similarity to this creature.

- For the past hundreds of years, he has been carrying a device made by craftsmen from planet Ix. The device recorded all the feelings and thoughts of Leto II. The records were discovered several millennia after the death of Leto II.

# Jessica Atreides

*Thufir Hawat: "The Duke did not marry you."*

*Jessica: "But he will not marry anyone else. Anyway, as long as I'm alive. "*

*- Jessica responds to suspicions of betrayal.*

Lady Jessica of the Atreides is the official concubine of the Duke Leto Atreides, the daughter of Baron Vladimir Harkonnen, the mother of Paul Atreides, she is also a representative of the Bene Gesserit order, who possessed rare beauty, fighting skills, hypnosis, manipulation of people and insight.

# Biography

Lady Jessica was born to unknown parents as part of the Bene Gesserit order's breeding program. She was raised to become the main concubine of the Duke of Leto Atreides. From the age of 14, Jessica was a servant of Gaius Helen Mohiam, who became her mentor in the order.

The leadership of the order ordered Jessica to give birth to Duke Leto's only daughters, one of whom would have to enter into a relationship with Feyd Rautha Harkonnen, from whom Kwisatz Hadarach was to appear). However, Jessica, out of love for the duke, violated the instructions and gave birth to his son Paul ("Jessica's crime"), and Kwisatz Hadarach appeared a generation earlier than planned. But to the annoyance of Bene Gesserit, they were unable to control him. Since childhood, Jessica has taught her son much secret knowledge of the order.

In 10191, the Reverend Mother Gaius Helen Mohiam arrived on Caladan to meet 15-year-old Paul and check him out. After some time, the entire House Atreides moved to a new planet, given to the house by the emperor for possession on condition of performing military, administrative service-Arrakis, also known as Dune. But there, the Atreides are trapped and fall victim to their deadly enemies — House Harkonnen. Duke Leto was killed, and

Jessica and her son managed to escape into the desert, as a result, they were considered dead, and House Atreides was completely destroyed.At the time of her escape, Jessica was pregnant with her second child, daughter Alia.

In the desert, the mother and son encounter the local inhabitants - Fremen warriors, adapted to survive in the desert. Through legends scattered by the Protective Ben-Geserite Missionary, they accept Paul and Jessica as the coming Mahdi (savior) and his mother. Paul and Jessica become members of the Fremen people, and Jessica is also a Reverend Mother of the tribe. To do this, she has to endure a spice agony, after which she acquires the memory of all her ancestors in the female line (at the same time, the embryo in her womb acquires the same memory). It also turns out that the person from whom Jessica's mother conceived her was Atreides' worst enemy - Baron Vladimir Harkonnen, who, despite his homosexual addictions, was seduced by one of the Bene Gesserit sisters.

After the victory of the Freman army in the battle of Arrakeen, Jessica returned to Caladan, a wet planet where the Atreides lived for many generations before moving to Arrakis. She returned to the Bene Gesserit order, and Gurney Halleck, an old confidant of the Duke of Leto, became her lover.

Ten years after the birth of Paul Atreides's children, the twins Leto and Ghanima, Jessica returns to Dune to look after her grandchildren and see if they could be taken under the control of the order. Leto II, thanks to his abilities, recognizes the name of Jessica's biological mother - Tanidia Nerus.

Realizing that her daughter Alia, the regent for her young nephews, is completely captured by the memories of her grandfather, Vladimir Harkonnen, who controls her actions, Jessica, having survived an attempt for your life, flew to the desert to sietch to Stilgar. A civil war broke out on Arrakis, which was raised by Fremen who rebelled against the tyranny of Alia and the greening of the planet started by Pardot Kynes. Alia's husband, ghola Duncan Idaho also realized that Alia was possessed, and when she gave him instructions to find Jessica, Duncan kidnapped her on the orders of The Preacher, a mystical figure from the desert.

Duncan takes her to Salusa Secundus, the home of the exiled House Corrino, where, on orders from The Preacher, Jessica is instructing Prince Farad'n Corrino in the Bene Gesserit ways. A few months later, Leto II removed Alia from power, and Prince Farad'n became the unofficial husband of Ghanima.

Lady Jessica passed away at the age of 102.

# Gurney Halleck

Gurney Halleck was the chief of the House Atreides military during the reign of Duke Leto Atreides, who was responsible for training and leading the House's army, as well as acting as a military instructor for the heir to Paul Atreides. He was a talented troubadour known for his baliset performance.

## Biography

Gurney Halleck was born on Giedi Prime. After his sister was enslaved, he tried to free her but got there himself. There, he tried to raise a riot for which his entire family was killed by representatives of House Harkonnen, led by the nephew of the Baron Glossu Rabban. Subsequently, he managed to escape and join the remnants of House Ix, whose heir, Rhombur Vernius, was at that time on Caladan.

After joining House Atreides, Halleck eventually became the chief of the House's armed forces. Thanks to his loyalty and other qualities, he became not only an approximate of the Duke of Leto but also a close friend to him and his official concubine lady Jessica.

During the stay of House Atreides on Caladan, Gurney Halleck, like Thufir Hawat, Duncan Idaho and Lady Jessica, was engaged in teaching the theory and practice of the martial art of the heir Paul Atreides, whom he also considered a close friend.

In 10191, House Atreides was given control of the planet Arrakis, where the Spice was extracted. Upon arrival on Arrakis with an elite military detachment, Halleck was sent by the duke to negotiate with the melangers who were going to leave the planet after the change of the ruling house and then to the smugglers to persuade both of them to cooperate with the Atreides, in which he achieved some success.

Gurney Halleck was one of the few House Atreides soldiers who survived the attack on the planet Arrakis by House Harkonnen and the Imperial Sardaukar. With a detachment of 74 people, he managed to get to the desert hideout of the smugglers and managed to convince one of their leaders, Staban Tuek to give them shelter. Tuek gave Halleck and his men a safe haven and persuaded him to postpone revenge on Harkonnen by staying with the smugglers. He also told Gurney that Thufir Hawat assumed that the fall of Atreides was due to the betrayal of Lady Jessica.

Over the next two years, he was engaged in Spice smuggling with Arrakis, and Halleck became a well-known and skilled smuggler. Once, when the smugglers, who were being pushed back by Harkonnen patrols into the deep desert, were ambushed by Fremen who imitated a large release of Spice on the sand, a battle ensued in which he was met by Paul Atreides, who by that time had become the leader of the Fremen and was called Muad'Dib.

Halleck told him that he had never left the service of Atreides, and together with the remaining smugglers, joined the Fremen who were preparing an uprising.

Upon arriving at the Sietch Tabr, Halleck nearly killed Jessica, whom he believed to be responsible for the death of Duke Leto, but Paul managed to convince him that Dr. Wellington Yueh was the traitor.

After the Padishah Emperor Shaddam Corrino IV was overthrown and Paul Atreides took over the Golden Lion Throne, the new emperor made Halleck the Earl of Caladan, a title comparable in status to his own father. Gurney moved to Caladan and developed a secret romantic relationship with Lady Jessica, who also lived here. He also retained the title of Baron Giedi Prime, abolished slavery on this planet and began to improve its infrastructure and ecology with the help of Caladan, including projects to restore planetary flora and fauna.

Subsequently, Halleck returned to Dune with Jessica, where he again established contact with smugglers.

## Personality

A talented troubadour, Halleck often played the nine-string baliset to entertain his guests or at the request of the Duke. He had very long fingers, capable of the most subtle movements, and these fingers often extracted very elegant music from the baliset. Gurney loved jokes, was very educated and at every opportunity quoted from many sources, and his quotes were very deep in content.

Halleck was ruthless and highly skilled but at the same time a noble warrior. He was the most loyal friend to those he loved and a terrible enemy to those he hated. He had outstanding melee skills.

# *Thufir Hawat*

Thufir Hawat is a mentat and Master of Assassins who served three generations of Atreides until Duke Leto was killed in an attack by House Harkonnen.

## Biography

Thufir Hawat was born on Logi, the third planet of the star Alpha Centauri B and was the first of nine sons of Golani and Alwidi Hawat. Golani Hawat, herself at one time trained as a potential mentat, recognized Thufir's outstanding abilities early on and provided him with training for the profession. Thufir continued his education at the School mentat on planet Ix.

Over time, Thufir Hawat has become one of the most formidable mentat in history. It was rumored that the padishah-Emperor Shaddam Corrino IV himself was afraid of him, which seems to be true since Shaddam demanded that Baron Vladimir Harkonnen kill Thufir.

During the relocation of House Atreides from Caladan to Arrakis, Thufir Hawat served as the head of House Security. After his subordinates allowed an attempt by Agent Harkonnen on the Duke's son, Paul Atreides, Hawat asked for resignation, but Duke Leto did not accept it.

After the death of Leto Atreides, Vladimir Harkonnen managed to make Hawat serve him, since with the loss of his duke, the only goal for Hawat was revenge against the padisha-emperor, who provided Harkonnen with several legions of Sardaukar, as well as revenge on Lady Jessica, whom he considered guilty of betrayal, which, in reality, was committed by Dr. Yueh. However, realizing that it is impossible to completely trust such a person, the baron ordered to give Thufir poison and then regularly give out an antidote along with food, that is, if Thufir had disappeared from the field of view of Harkonnen, he would have died in a few days.

Shortly before the overthrow of House Harkonnen, he was tried to force the murder of Paul Atreides, but Thufir preferred death to betrayal.

# *Duncan Idaho*

Duncan Idaho - House Atreides weaponsmith.

## Appearance

Duncan had a feline fluidity of movement. Tall, swarthy, with deep-set eyes and curly black hair, he was popular with women. During the service with the Duke of Leto, Idaho was sent if it was necessary to follow the lady or find out information from her.

## Biography

Born and lived on Giedi Prime until his parents were arrested and killed by Glossu Rabban. He fled to Caladan and trained at the House Ginaz Weaponsmith Academy. He died on Arrakis, defending Paul Atreides and his mother Lady Jessica from sardaukar, taking the lives of 19 opponents.

Subsequently, Bene Tleilax resurrected him, and Duncan became ghola Hayt-personal mentat Muad'Dib. Having regained his memory, he married Alia, the sister of Muad'Dib.

# House Harkonnen

## *Vladimir Harkonnen*

Vladimir Harkonnen, more often referred to simply as Baron, representative of House Harkonnen, ruler of the planet Giedi Prime.

His mentat is Piter de Vries.

## Biography

In her youth, Baron was seduced by a follower of Bene Gesserit, and as a result, she had a daughter, Lady Jessica.

Baron was killed during the Arrakis Revolt by his young granddaughter Alia Atreides with the help of Gom Jabbar. His title passed for a few hours to the heir of the Baron, Feyd-Rautha Harkonnen.

## Appearance And Character

A huge man, monstrously fat, so much so that his obese body is supported by portable forcefield generators on a special harness so that he could carry his weight, which was at least two hundred kilograms. He had black spider eyes swollen with fat, plump lips, and pink fat cheeks that shake when walking. Multiple chins. Fat hands and palms with thick fingers, usually studded with rings. Fat shoulders. The voice is a booming, thick bass.

## Family Ties

Vladimir Harkonnen is a direct male descendant of bashar Abulurd Harkonnen, who was expelled for cowardice after The Battle of Corrin.

Vladimir's only known child is Lady Jessica; therefore, he is the grandfather of Paul and Alia Atreides. Baron Vladimir did not have a direct heir, but there were two nephews — Glossu Rabban and Feyd-Rautha Harkonnen, the elder he makes the ruler of Arrakis and the younger his successor, na-baron.

# *Glossu Rabbit*

Glossu Rabbit, also known as Beast — is the eldest nephew of Baron Vladimir Harkonnen. Twice appointed regent-siridar Arrakis.

## Position On The Dune

Glossu inherited Harkonnen's characteristic cruelty and sadistic tendencies but did not possess their typical cunning. He earned the nickname "Beast" by killing his father, Abulurd Rabban. Being called to the court of the Baron, he took the surname Harkonnen.

Glossu Rabban was notorious for his brutal and incompetent rule on Arrakis, both during the time when Dune was the fiefdom of Harkonnen and during the Fremen uprising led by Muad'Dib. The baron allowed Glossu to terrorize Arrakis so that his younger nephew, Feyd-Rautha Harkonnen, could act as the savior of the people from the terrible terror of the Rabban.

According to the plan proposed by mentat Thufir Hawat, in the conditions of the outbreak of the uprising on Arrakis, the baron actually stopped sending military aid to his nephew, forcing him to switch from attack to defense, which somewhat eased the oppression in some villages of the hollows and unsuccessfully tried to conclude a truce with the Fremen. However, Baron Harkonnen's plan failed due to the appearance of Muad'Dib.

Glossu Rabban died in 10193 PG during the Battle of Arrakeen.

## Appearance And Character Traits

Glossu Rabban was short, plump, although still quite flexible, with a broad face, in which the ancestral features of Harkonnen on the male line were clearly visible — close-set eyes and massive shoulders.

Rabban did not have the insight and cunning of his uncle and his younger brother but was demonstratively cruel in achieving goals and dismissive of others.

# *Feyd-Rautha Harkonnen*

Feyd-Rautha Harkonnen is one of the antagonists of the book "Dune." Feyd was the young nephew of Vladimir Harkonnen from House Harkonnen. He was a significant figure in the Baron's plans to achieve power. Vladimir Harkonnen appointed him as the na-baron of House Harkonnen.

Baron appreciated the young Feyd-Rautha more than his older brother "Beast" Glossu Rabbit. Feyd was both intelligent and charismatic, and also Harkonnen-like cruel and sadistic, although the latter was associated with his upbringing. Feyd was killed by Paul Atreides during the kanly act shortly after the Arrakis Revolt.

# Early Years

Born under the name Feyd-Rautha Rabban. His father was Abu-lurd Rabban, and his mother was Emmi. Feyd's father hoped that his younger son would become a worthy successor and would not inherit the dishonorable fame of House Harkonnen, unlike the older, more cruel son, Glossu.

Feyd was named after his maternal grandfather, Rautha Rabban, who was killed on the orders of Glossu. When Baron heard about this, he decided to take Feyd from his father and raise him on Giedi Prime as a potential heir. It was then that his last name was changed to Harkonnen.

## Role In The Breeding Program

Feyd, like Paul Atreides, was part of a centuries-old breeding program conducted by the Bene Gesserit Order, which planned a family union between the son of Harkonnen and the daughter of Atreides in order to unite the Great Houses once and for all to end the enmity between them. Their son could very likely be Kwisatz Haderach.

Therefore, Jessica Atreides' decision to ignore the requirements of the order and give birth to a son to the duke caused the need to confront Feyd and Paul as heirs of the warring noble houses. The death of each of them meant the collapse of the breeding program that had been carried out for several millennia. For this reason, Bene Gesserit used Margot Fenring to give birth to a child from Feyd to preserve his genetic chain.

## Role In House Harkonnen

The Baron was planning a strategically important family alliance, hoping to marry Feyd-Rautha to Princess Irulan Corrino, the eldest daughter of Emperor Shaddam IV to give Harkonnen power over the Empire. To strengthen Feyd's position, the Baron wanted to appoint him as the head of Arrakis after the tyranny and chaos arranged by Glossu Rabbit, which allowed Feyd to be presented as the savior of the people.

Ambition and a passionate desire for the baronial title allowed Feyd to become a victim of the manipulations of Thufir Hawat, a former adviser to Atreides, captured by the Baron. As a result, both the Baron and his heir were soon killed.

# Piter de Vries

Piter de Vries is a vicious mentat created by Bene Tleilax and served as House Harkonnen during the time of Baron Vladimir Harkonnen.

## Biography

Piter de Vries was an outstanding mentat for his cunning and insidious nature, cultured by Bene Tleilax, and characterized by immoral sadistic tendencies. Even though Harkonnen lost his possessions on Arrakis, Piter's mentat abilities and considerable intelligence told him that Vladimir Harkonnen planned to kill him soon, but he remained loyal to House Harkonnen and enthusiastically served the Baron. Moreover, realizing his indispensability, de Vries allowed himself such liberties in conversations with the Baron for which any other servant would have been immediately killed, believing that he could calculate the moment when the Baron would decide to get rid of him.

Among his achievements was finding a way to bypass the Imperial Conditioning of the doctor from Suk School, who had previously considered an absolute guarantee against betrayal. He found that it is possible to control the behavior of such a doctor at will if you hold a loved one hostage. This method was successfully implemented against Dr. Wellington Yueh, who was forced by Harkonnen to commit treason against the House Atreides, which he served. De Vries kidnapped Wellington's wife and killed her but convinced the doctor that she was still alive. To save his wife from suffering at the hands of Harkonnen, Yueh disabled the castle's defensive shields and handed the Duke of Leto Atreides and into the hands of Harkonnen soldiers, after which he was stabbed by de Vries.

Another achievement of de Vries was a residual poison that he developed, which is not recognizable by conventional means: a person poisoned by him must regularly receive an antidote in food; otherwise he would face a quick death.

For the successful plan to defeat the Atreides, Baron Harkonnen promised de Vries the duke's concubine, Lady Jessica. However, when Lady Jessica was in the hands of the Baron, he offered Piter a choice: either this woman and exile from the borders of the Empire or the duchy belonging to Atreides, which he could rule on behalf of the Baron at his discretion; that is, become the Duke of Arrakis in everything but the title. De Vries agreed to the dukedom, not realizing that the Baron was only playing with him.

After Duke Leto was captured, he was taken to the Harkonnen lighter, where he was interrogated by Vladimir Harkonnen and Piter de Vries. During the interrogation, the duke bit through an artificial tooth inserted by Dr. Yueh and exhaled the poison contained in it. As a result of the attempt, Piter de Vries, who was next to Leto, was killed, but Vladimir Harkonnen managed to survive.

## Personality And Character Traits

Piter de Vries was an elegant, frail, short man with hawk-like features, a somewhat effeminate appearance and a pleasant, musical-sounding tenor. Due to the use of a large amount of spice, Piter had characteristic blue-on-blue eyes.

De Vries was an ambitious and impatient sadist, with viciousness comparable to Baron. The only mistake in his calculations was that Lady Jessica gave birth to a son to the Duke of Leto and not a daughter, as he assumed.

# Imperial House Corrino

## *Shaddam Corrino IV*

Shaddam Corrino IV - Padishah Emperor of the Known Universe, 81st in his dynasty.

## Biography

Crowned to the throne of the Golden Lion in 10156 PG, when his father Elrud IX was poisoned by the poison of Murky.

During the first sixteen years of his reign, the number of burseg (general-commanders of the Sardaukar) doubled. And the funding for Sardaukar's training has been steadily declining for the last thirty years before Arrakis Revolt. Excessive passion for palace duties and excessive pomposity of the court led to an economic and political imbalance in the Empire, accompanied by the growth of the authority of House Atreides among the Great Houses of the Landsraad (assembly of the Great Houses of the Empire, the supreme legislative body of the Empire).

In an effort to eliminate the potential danger from Atreides, Shaddam entered into a secret conspiracy with the head of the longstanding and most consistent opponent of Atreides, House Harkonnen.

When the Fremen launched a war against the Harkonnens, resulting in significantly reduced production of Spice. Shaddam IV personally flew to Arrakis, but his troops and the Harkonnen troops suffered a crushing defeat from the rebels led by Muad'Dib.

Shaddam IV himself and his court were captured, and the Padishah emperor was forced to abdicate the throne and agree to the marriage of his eldest daughter Irulan with Muad'Dib.

In 10196 PG, he officially abdicated and established a regency in favor of his daughter Irulan, retiring with his court to exile on the planet Salusa Secundus, where he died in 10202 PG.

## Appearance And Character Traits

Shaddam IV had a narrow face and icy eyes, a gaze which resembled the gaze of a bird of prey.

# *Irulan Corrino*

Irulan Corrino is the eldest daughter of the Padishah Emperor Shaddam IV, a pupil of the Bene Gesserit order, a writer. The official wife of the Emperor Paul Atreides.

## Biography

Irulan was born when her father was already 57 years old. Her mother Anirul, a member of the Bene Gesserit Sisters of the Hidden Order, taught her daughter the well-known techniques of the order from childhood. Irulan had four sisters, and she is the eldest. She, her sisters and her mother had to spy on her father, especially when a slave concubine was brought to him for their own safety — the intrigues never stopped, the purpose of which was the birth of an heir to the emperor. In addition, women had to learn to avoid sophisticated murder weapons perfectly. According to Irulan, their father was also involved in some of these attempts.

When Irulan was fourteen, the girl learned that her father secretly wanted to be related to the Duke of Leto Atreides and loudly expressed regret that Irulan was not older at the time when the duke was choosing a wife.

In 10193 PG, immediately after the army of the Fremen defeated the troops of the Houses of Harkonnen and Corrino, during the official ceremony of surrender, Irulan and Gaius Helen Mohiam managed to convince the padishah-emperor to give the princess in marriage to Paul Atreides: Bene Gesserit was reminded of the agreement to put a pupil of the order on the throne and that it was the Irulan who were preparing for this. Paul agreed to the marriage, but warned Irulan that the union would be purely political and childless.

## The Emperor's Wife

In 10196, a regency was established with a nominal transfer of power from Shaddam IV to Irulan: Paul Atreides received full real power in the Empire, and Irulan became part of the Imperial Council, but never received the formal status of empress. In the same year, Irulan's mother died.

After becoming the new emperor, Paul Atreides did not deviate from formal relations with Irulan, giving his love only to the official concubine Chani. In an effort to prevent Paul from giving birth to an heir, Irulan constantly secretly added a contraceptive to Chani's food. Irulan herself had permission for extramarital affairs but the strictest prohibition on conceiving a child as a result of them. Engaged in her favorite literary activity since her youth, Irulan wrote a large number of books, a significant part of which was dedicated to Paul Muad'Dib.

By 10205 PG, a conspiracy had matured among the opponents

of the emperor Paul Atreides, one of the key figures of which was Irulan: one of the main motivations for participation was her desire to start a new imperial dynasty. At the same time, playing a double game, Irulan warned the emperor about a conspiracy involving a part of the Fremen. When Irulan's role in the Chani poisoning was revealed, she demanded the death of the princess, but Paul Atreides denied her this.

## Appearance And Character Traits

Irulan Corrino was a tall, blond woman with chiseled features of an elongated face and green eyes. Her whole appearance speaks of high birth, radiating a truly classic arrogance. She was arrogant and proud.

After many years of living on Arrakis, the princess' body had become more lean, and her eyes had acquired the color of Ibad.

# *Farad'n Corrino*

Farad'n Corrino is the heir of House Corrino. Consort of the Empress Ghanima Atreides. Grandson of Shaddam Corrino IV.

## Biography

Farad'n Corrino was born in the family of Dalak Fenring and Wensicia Corrino, the daughter of the 81st Padishah Emperor Shaddam IV. Farad'n was raised on the planet Salusa Secundus.

The domineering and ambitious mother of Farad'n intended to use her talented son to return the Golden Lion Throne to her House, so she provided him with an appropriate upbringing for this task. Farad'n studied law and the art of management, as well as philosophy. He carefully studied the House Atreides' control system, hoping to find out how they managed to defeat Corrino and reproduced some such developments. Fearing the influence of Bene Gesserit, Wensicia excluded her son from the curriculum of studying with the sisters of the order.

## Personality And Character Traits

Farad'n Corrino had a sullen face with heavy brow ridges and a stubbornly compressed firm mouth.

By the age of eighteen, masculinity begins to emerge in Farad'n's features, and he began to resemble his grandfather Shaddam IV.

Farad'n by nature had a quick, inquisitive, perceptive mind. At times, he became withdrawn, and it became unclear what was on his mind.

Political activity both attracted and repelled the prince. Over time, he became imbued with a thirst for power, but he did not lose interest in history and literature.

Farad'n treated his teacher Tyekanik with respect, but over time, he began to distance himself from his mother and eventually, ruthlessly removed her from power.

# *Hasimir Fenring*

Hasimir Fenring-mentat assassin, advisor and closest friend of the Padishah Emperor Shaddam Corrino IV. The husband of Lady Margot Fenring.

Hasimir Fenring was a genetic eunuch, and only this prevented him from becoming a Kwisatz Haderach, a product of the centuries-old eugenic program of the Bene Gesserit Order.

Fenring was raised together with the future Padishah-emperor Shaddam IV, and when his childhood friend took over the Golden Lion Throne, he became his closest adviser and only true friend.

Over time, Hasimir became one of the best fighters of the Empire. It was Count Fenring who helped with the help of chaumurky (a kind of poison) to get rid of Elrood IX, the predecessor of Shaddam IV on the imperial throne. He also carried out other delicate orders of the emperor, for example, he was engaged in the selection of concubine slaves for him.

Despite the inability to have children, Hasimir Fenring took as his lawful wife a pupil of the Bene Gesserit order, Lady Margot Fenring, with whom he had a close relationship and who was a loyal companion to him.

## Appearance And Character Traits

Count Hasimir Fenring was a rather ugly man of short stature with a marten-like face and huge dark green eyes, who looked shifty and sneaky. He was considered a big dandy.

The count was able to successfully hide his outstanding fighting abilities from observers, masterfully portraying a weakling; in conversation, the movements of his hands or the turn of his head could say one thing, and his remarks could say the opposite, so it was impossible to understand what the count was really thinking.

Hasimir Fenring and his wife knew a secret language that allowed them to transmit important information directly during a conversation with third parties using interjections.

The Earl was well-disposed towards House Atreides, although after their defeat, he believed that it was not worth spending grief on losers.

Paul Muad'Dib, having acquired the gift of prophecy, has never been able to see Hasimir Fenring in visions of the future.

# Fremen

## *Stilgar*

Stilgar Ben Fifrawi-male Freeman, Naib Sietch Tabr and head of the Council of Fremen Chiefs, one of the closest associates of Paul Muad'Dib, uncle of Chani Kynes.

## Biography

After becoming a respected freman in Sietch Tabr and realizing that he could become his Naib, Stilgar, according to tradition, challenged the previous Naib, who was his friend and with whom Stilgar shared many dangers, and defeated him.

In 10191, when the Padishah-Emperor Shaddam Corrino IV gave the planet Arrakis to the Duke of Leto Atreides, the duke's close swordmaster Duncan Idaho, sent to Arrakis to study the Fremen and establish trust relations with them, met with Stilgar. Idaho earned the respect of Stilgar and other Fremen for his bravery and adherence to traditions.

After the Duke's arrival on Arrakis, Idaho, who considered Stilgar a fine example of a freeman-naib, brought him to the palace, and during a meeting with Leto, Stilgar agreed to Duncan serving both Sietch Tabr and the duke at the same time.

After House Atreides fell as a result of a massive attack by House Harkonnen and the Imperial Sardukar, the Duke's heir Paul Atreides and his mother Jessica, who had fled to the desert, came across a detachment of Stilgar in the Tuono Basin. Stilgar insisted on taking Paul under the protection of the tribe.

## Personality And Character Traits

Stilgar was an outstanding Fremen leader who earned great respect from his people. Having a flexible mind, he was able to combine adherence to ancient traditions and the ability to reject dogmas when evaluating the actions of other people. Even after becoming the emperor's confidant, he still retained the features of a "wild" freeman.

Stilgar was tall, with a thin nose, full-lipped mouth, black hair and a black beard. Since childhood, consuming food with a high content of Spice, like all Freemen, he had blue-on-blue ibad eyes.

Stilgar had several wives.

# *Chani Kynes*

Chani Kynes, Sihaya — Fremen woman, lover, then concubine of Duke Paul Atreides, daughter of Liet Kynes, mother of twins Ghanima and Leto Atreides II.

## Biography

Paul sees Chani in his prophetic dreams long before they meet. After the fall of the Atreides house on the Dune, Paul and his mother escape to the desert, where Chani becomes Paul's lover, and subsequently his concubine and wife among the Fremen.

Twelve years later, Irulan, obeying the orders of Bene Gesserit, regularly secretly adds Chani contraceptives to food that has already lost a child once. Chani turns to the Fremen for help and gets a remedy that increases the chance of getting pregnant, and soon it happens. But she dies when she gives birth to her children, the twins Ghanima and Leto Atreides II. Twenty years later, despite her death, Chani lives as part of another memory and almost completely takes over the personality of Ghanima. Leto II manages to save his sister from this.

Hundreds of years later, Chani as part of another memory still lives in Leto II. At one point, he lets Chani speak through him.

# Liet-Kynes

Liet-Kynes-Imperial planetary ecologist, Freeman, nephew of Stilgar, son of Pardot Kynes. Chani's father.

## Origin

Born in 10154 PG. According to his origin, Liet-Kynes was only half a Freeman since his father was originally from Salusa Secundus.

Liet's mother, Frith, was the sister of Stilgar, the future Naib of Sietch Tabr. Under his upbringing, Liet adopted the traditions of the Fremen society and became a wormriding from his youth.

After the death of his father, Liet-Kynes inherited his position as the planetary ecologist of Arrakis, while being the leader of the Fremen and also continued to carry out his father's secret business-preparing for the terraforming of the planet.

## Role In The Conflict

When Dune was transferred to the ownership of House Atreides, Liet became an assistant to the Duke of Leto, although at first he did not think to support him. However, after the duke risked his life and the life of his son Paul and saved the lives of workers, showing that for him, human losses are incomparable with the losses of machinery and spices. He also sees that they have one goal - changing the face of the Dune so that it becomes suitable for people; Kynes took his side.

Kynes was captured by Harkonnen after Paul and Jessica's escape arranged by him. Since Kynes was an imperial official, it was dangerous to kill him, so on the orders of Harkonnen, he was taken and abandoned in the deep desert with a damaged stillsuit (which, in the conditions of the Dune, meant certain death) in order to take away suspicion of his death from himself.

# Otheym

Otheym-a male freeman, Fedaykin Paul Atreides during the war against House Harkonnen.

## Biography

Otheym belonged to the Sietch Gara Kulon, and after Paul Muad'dib called the Fremen to war against Harkonnen, Otheym responded to his call and became one of the first Fedaykin. By his actions, he earned the trust of Muad'dib. Otheym was responsible for the safety of Paul and his family in Sietch Tabr, while he was in a trance, having drunk the unconverted Water of Life (liquid secretions of a sandworm during its death in the water).

After Paul came out of his trance, Otheym overheard a conversation between him and his family, convincing him that Muad'dib was truly Lisan al Gaib, a man who can look into the depths of Water of Life like a Reverend Mother. He told it to the whole tribe. During the liberation of Arrakis from Harkonnen, Otheym was one of the senior commanders of the rebels.

During the jihad Muad'dib, Otheym fought on many different planets. During the fighting, he was seriously wounded — after it, the entire left side of his face consisted of intersecting scars, and after the victory at Tarahell, he contracted splitting disease (an incurable disease that leads to skin damage and severe coughing attacks).

Upon his return to Arrakis, Otheym settled in the suburb of Arrakeen, a new neighborhood built for jihad veterans, where he lived with his wife Dhuri and daughter Lichna. Relatives invited the best and expensive doctors to him, but splitting disease could not be cured, and Otheym was slowly dying ...

## Personality And Character Traits

Otheym had a massive head with a wide, flat face and a long hooked nose.

By his last days, Otheym was wearing false teeth made of silver metal.

In Otheym's house in Arrakeen, a narrow shelf hung on the wall, occupied by a series of portraits. Most of them depicted bearded Fremen, some of whom were in stillsuit, and in other portraits, imperial uniforms sparkled against the background of exotic landscapes of other worlds, most often sea.

# Bene Gesserit

## *Gaius Helen Mohiam*

Gaius Helen Mohiam was the senior proctor of the Bene Gesserit School on Wallach IX when she took young Jessica, the daughter of Baron Vladimir Harkonnen, as a student. Over the years of training, Jessica began to have mixed feelings for her mentor — she loved her, but at the same time, hated her for the suffering she caused. Later, when she became a concubine of Duke Leto Atreides, Jessica gave birth to a son, not a daughter, and Gaius Helen Mohiam was angry her former student's willfulness.

## Appearance And Character Traits

By the time House Atreides moved to Arrakis, Gaius Helen was an old, heavy, wrinkled woman. She had gray hair that could shade her face like a hood and shiny, like a bird's, dark eyes that turned blue due to the use of Spice. She had pale gums and silvery metal teeth. Her voice was harsh and raspy," sounding like an out-of-tune baliset."

Despite Jessica's first defection, Gaius Helen Mohiam continued to love her as a daughter. Gaius Helen Mohiam herself was heartily hated by Paul Atreides, ready to kill her if it were not for the political expediency of the opposite.

## Skills

Gaius Helen Mohiam had the skills of mind reading and mind

penetration.

## Bene Gesserit

1. Anirul, Bene Gesserit of Hidden Rank.
2. Bellonda is a Reverend Mother and the chief Mentat-Archivist counselor in Heretics of Dune.
3. Quintinius Violet Chenoeh, specially trained as an oral recorder.
4. Hesterion is one of the few sisters with access to sensitive breeding records.
5. Ramallo is a Fremen Reverend Mother in the tribe who take in Paul Atreides and Lady Jessica after the Harkonnen attack.
6. Wanna, wife of Dr. Wellington Yueh, Suk doctor.

# Spacing Guild

Spacing Guild

1. Norma Cenva, inventor of foldspace technology; first Guild Navigator
2. Edric, Navigator in the events of Dune Messiah
3. Edrik, Navigator in the events of Hunters of Dune and Sandworms of Dune
4. D'murr Pilru, Guild Navigator, twin brother of C'tair Pilru of Ix
5. Aurelius Venport, founder of VenKee enterprises, the ancestor of the Guild
6. Adrien Venport, son of Aurelius Venport and Norma Cenva

# Thinking machines

## Thinking Machines

1. Chirox, reprogrammed by humans, used as a trainer on Ginaz.
2. Erasmus, independent robot.
3. Gilbertus Albans, adopted human-son of Erasmus; founder of the Order of Mentats.
4. Omnius, the Evermind; leader of the machines.
5. Seurat, co-pilot to Vorian Atreides.

# TECHNOLOGIES

## *Ghola*

Ghola - a clone, is an artificial creature that is grown in an axolotl vat from genetic material obtained from the cells of a deceased creature in the fictional Dune universe created by Frank Herbert. The Tleilaxu initially had a monopoly on this biotechnological process, but in Herbert's later books, the Bene Gesserit also use this technology.

The Bene Tleilaxu controlled their creatures by hypnotizing them with a special predetermined sound (often a humming or whistling noise).

## Appearances

The first ghola to appear in the book series - Hayt from Messiah of Dune - is the reincarnation of Duncan Idaho. Later, gholas were taught to grow from just a few cages, as was the case with subsequent Idaho gholas, which were later granted to Leto II in God-Emperor of Dune.

Before the events of Messiah of Dune, gholas were only physical copies without memory of their original incarnations. Ghola Hayt was programmed by the Tleilaxu to kill Paul Atreides under post-hypnotic direction. Contrary to the expectations of the Tleilaxu, the assassination attempt failed because the stress of trying to kill someone to whom the ghola was deeply devoted in a previous life breaks the intellectual barrier between the ghola's consciousness and the living memory of its original incarnation. Hayt returns the memory of the once-living Idaho, and he becomes the reincarnation of the latter.

This discovery is of great importance to the Tleilaxu Masters, who subsequently use the axlotl tank and memory recovery technologies to achieve immortality. Each Master is recreated after his death, and his memory is returned to him. Thus, he accumulates knowledge and experience of many generations, which allows him to make plans for many millennia.

In "God Emperor of Dune" for Leto II, the gholas of Idaho's permanent companion are recreated over and over again, returning to him the memory of the original Idaho (but not the memory of his previous gholas). In this novel, Idaho gholas are perfect reincarnations, obtained from just "a few cells" and are created within just 1-2 years.

In Heretics of Dune, the Bene Gesserit becomes the owner of Duncan Idaho's ghola. Interestingly, when he regains his memory, it affects all his reincarnations, including even those gholas whose cells are no longer available. This suggests some supernatural forces that are not explained in any way in the novels.

# Thinking Machines

Thinking machines are intelligent mechanisms that were created by people and eventually began to dominate them. The revolt of humans against machines, known as the Butlerian Jihad, is a turning point in the prehistory of the Dune Universe.

## The Original Dune Book Series

**In the Dune Dictionary-the following definition is given:**

> *«JIHAD, BUTLERIAN: (also The Great Revolt) - a holy war against computers, thinking machines and robots endowed with consciousness, which began in 201 DG and ended in 108 DG. Its main commandment, "Do not create a machine in the image and likeness of a human" is reflected in the Orange Catholic Bible.»*

**In "The Messiah of Dune" (1969), the Tleilaxu face dancer Scytale remarks:**

> *«Since the days of the Butlerian Jihad, when "thinking machines" were wiped off the face of most of the universe, computers have inspired distrust.»*

Frank Herbert repeatedly mentions thinking machines and Jihad in his later Dune novels but does not go into much detail about how he imagined them. The death of the writer in 1986 left the topic undisclosed and free for guesses.

# Legends Of Dune

In 2002, Brian Herbert and Kevin Anderson published the first novel in the Legends of Dune backstory series.

In describing the Butlerian Jihad, Legends of Dune sheds light on the essence of thinking machines.

# Criticism And Reviews

The magazine "World of Fantastic" put Omnius in second place in the list of "10 human-computer conflicts" (First place went to the conflict of human-computers in the Matrix), noting that having thrown off the yoke of thinking machines, people became dependent on spice.

# *Stillsuit*

Stillsuit is a distillation suit that allows you to retain, process and reuse body moisture in the harsh desert conditions of the planet Arrakis. A well-functioning stillsuit allowed the owner to survive in the open desert for a week.

## Description

The stillsuit was invented on Arrakis and was a tight-fitting jumpsuit that usually covered the entire body, up to the neck and wrists. In addition to the stillsuit, gloves were worn on the hands, but to carry out fine work, the fremen took them off, at the same time rubbing their hands with creosote bush leaves, which prevented moisture from evaporating through the skin of the hands.

Its thin, multi-layered fabric was designed to dissipate heat, as well as filter and cool the water released from the body — sweat and other secretions. The water recycled by the overalls was collected in special pockets and was available for reuse through a tube.

If the overalls were well fitted, the person in it lost only one sip of water a day.

## Interesting Facts

- During the reign of House Harkonnen on Arrakis, the Fremen refused to sell their highly effective stillsuit to its representatives, which greatly complicated the Harkonnen activities in the deserts of Arrakis.

- After Paul Atreides became emperor, some courtiers who knew about the role of Fremen in his rise began to wear a stillsuit under their clothes, which amused the emperor. When it turned out that their costumes were non-functional imitations, their owners became objects of ridicule and stopped this practice, but this fashion resumed under Emperor Leto II.

# Holtzman effect

The Holtzman effect is a fictional scientific phenomenon in the Dune universe created by Frank Herbert.

In keeping with the Legend of Dune prequel trilogy, written by Brian Herbert and Kevin Anderson, the Holtzmann effect is named after its discoverer, Tio Holtzman (although it is known that Holtzman actually used the merits of his assistant, Norma Cenva, for many applications of his discovery). This phenomenon has not been detailed in the books, but it is known to exploit the surrounding subatomic energy fields, enabling the creation of protective force shields, instant space travel, and other practical applications.

In different books, Frank Herbert used different spellings for the name of the phenomenon. Thus, in different books, it can be found both as Holtzman, Holtzmann and Holzmann. The author must have done this on purpose, judging by the fact that he often changed the spelling of terms and proper names in events separated by huge periods of time in which the events of the Dune universe unfold, thus making it clear that languages, civilizations and cultures change over time. ... So, for example, Arrakis eventually becomes Rakis, and Giedi Prime is reduced to Gammu.

## Holtzman Shield

By the time of the events described in the first book of Dune, when thinking machines no longer posed a threat, this technology was used to create personal protective shields. Unlike other similar ones in science fiction, these shields are not a spherical projection of force but are energy fields corresponding to the shape of a streamlined object, allowing other objects to penetrate, only moving at allowed speeds. Given that the creature using the shield is not able to breathe in it (the restriction on the penetration rate also applies to atmospheric gases), personal shields are configured for a relatively high penetration rate, from 6 to 9 cm/sec. And the shields used to protect ships and planetary installations often allow only extremely low penetration rates since it is possible to use artificial life support technologies inside them with a working shield, which is not possible in personal shields.

Early enough, Cenva figured out that if a beam thrower hit the Holtzman shield, an explosive reaction of subatomic fusion would occur, that is, a nuclear explosion. The center of the explosion becomes a random point, which, in one case, appears inside the shield, in another in a laser weapon, and in the third, in both. Therefore, the use of laser weapons in shielded areas can cause a military disaster and damage the environment.

The Holtzman Shield is an effective scientific method: it makes it impossible to use weapons with directed energy against any standing enemy, and, moreover, makes the usual firearms and missiles useless, bringing a medieval atmosphere to the narrative and forcing the use of melee weapons, although the action takes place in the distant future.

The only planet where the Holtzman Shield is not widely used is Arrakis. The field generator appears to generate frequent vibrations that infuriate any sandworm. Thus, firearms become useful again on Dune. Even ancient artillery can be effective.

## Holtzman Drive

In the case of the Holtzman Drive, the Holtzman effect is used to fold space at a quantum level, which allows Space Guild ships to instantly cover not only the distances between stars but even much larger distances over which space empires stretch.

However, the chaotic and seemingly indefinable quantum nature of the "folded space" requires at least Guild Navigator intervention. Otherwise, the complex mathematics involved in calculating a reliable physical projection of displacement events can only be calculated by high-tech thinking machines, which were strictly forbidden after the Butlerian Jihad.

In order to anticipate upcoming events and avoid a collision of a ship with a space body, the Guild, saturating creatures with Spice vapors, creates navigators. Spice gives navigators the ability to intuitively "see safe paths through folded space."

## Similar Ideas In Science Fiction

1. Technology similar to the Holtzmann shield has been used in the Stargate universe.

2. The personal force fields in Charles Harness' novel The Paradox Men (1954) stop fast bullets but let slow rapiers pass.

# Distrans

Distrans is a device for imposing a temporary neuro imprint on the nervous system of a living being.

## Description

As a rule, distrans were implanted only in lower animals — tame birds or bats (cielago). The cry of the animal was modulated by the imprint so that it carried a given message, which can then be deciphered by the addressee using another distran. Distrans meant you didn't have to encrypt the message, everything in it was determined by the finest shades of natural sounds, captured in all their complexity.

Distrans were used on Arrakis for communication in the Desert (and were often more effective than radio communication, due to the high level of static interference).

By the time of the end of Muad'Dib's Jihad, politicians and officials of the Atreides Empire were widely using devices implanted in people (for example, in the adrenal cortex) for the security of correspondence.

# Lasgun

Lasgun is a continuous (non-pulse) laser, which was used as a weapon in the Empire.

## Description

Lasguns were emitters of continuous light, its white or blue fire rays, emitted with a buzzing sound, burned through any known materials, if they were not protected by a force field.

As a rule, combat lasguns were made in the form of a pistol or a rifle and were also mounted on ornithopters (including turret installations). Lasguns were very expensive and difficult to maintain weapons.

The interaction of the beam of this weapon with the Holtzman Shield led to a subatomic reaction and a thermonuclear explosion. The magnitude of this explosion was unpredictable: sometimes, it destroyed only targets inside the field and a person with a weapon and sometimes the explosion could be more powerful than an atomic one.

# ORGANIZATIONS

## *Bene Gesserit*

Bene Gesserit is an ancient (and first) school of body and mind training, originally created by women after the Great Jihad destroyed the so-called Thinking Machines and robots.

### Eugenic Program

For many centuries, the Bene Gesserit have been engaged in a selective genetic program, in which all major dynasties participated. The Bene Gesserit have literally nurtured key genetic lines and are trying to preserve them. The Bene Gesserit teaching was founded by those who saw the need for continuity in the life of mankind; they understood that it was impossible without a division into humans and animals — for their eugenic programs. They may plan the birth of a child by a ward from someone from close relatives to consolidate the dominant in the genetic line or for other reasons.

To fulfill its main goal (namely, the breeding of Kwisatz Haderach), the order carefully monitored two genetic lines: House Atreides and House Harkonnen.

All records of the eugenic program of human mating are stored in the Marriage Index.

# Kwisatz Haderach

Kwisatz Haderach - as Bene Gesserit called the Unknown, who they wanted to get with the help of genetics and eugenics - a male Bene Gesserit, whose natural mental abilities would allow him to embrace space and time. In other words, to have access to the genetic memory of all ancestors in the male and female lines and have the gift of foresight and other psychic abilities.

Simply put, they needed a person whose mind would allow them to understand and use higher-order dimensions. They wanted to create a super-machine, a living computer endowed with prophetic abilities.

Based on centuries of research, the sisters concluded that when crossing two strong genetic lines — Atreides and Harkonnens — Kwisatz Haderach can be bred with a high probability. As a tool for this task, Bene Gesserit Jessica, the daughter of Baron Vladimir Harkonnen, who became the concubine of the Duke of Leto, was introduced into the House of Atreides. She received an order to give birth to the duke's daughter, who in the future will have to marry the nephew of the baron Vladimir - Feyd-Rautha. The probability of obtaining Kwisatz Haderach from the combination of these genes was very high.

However, Lady Jessica ruined the plans of the order by giving birth to a son to the duke, and thus personally gave birth to Kwisatz Haderach without the knowledge of the sisters.

# Impact Of Bene Gesserit

The policy pursued by Bene Gesserit is very prudent and comprehensive. The Order wants to control as many aspects of the life of the inhabited universe as possible, as well as to influence and react in time to various kinds of events.

Bene Gesserit is a non-voting partner of Combine Honnete Ober Advancer Mercantiles.

## Bene Gesserit School

The Bene Gesserit Maternal School Center is located on Wallach IX. The pupils of the school are young girls. The term of study is 14 years. Not every girl can be trained in this school - only those who descend from the sister of Bene Gesserit and those whose genetic code will satisfy the leadership of the order. Many of the students do not know anything about their origin, but their genetic lines are recorded in the books of the school.

Only the Reverend Mother can become the Head of the Bene Gesserit Regional School.

One of the first and obligatory things taught in the Bene Gesserit School is the languages - bhotani jib, chakobsa and others.

It is known that one of the courses of lectures at the School was "Espionage and counter-espionage."

## The Bene Gesserit Way

The Bene Gesserit way is the art of observing the smallest details.

## Secrets Of Bene Gesserit

Adepts of the Bene Gesserit Order are taught various types of skills, from combat skills to self-control methods. Their special skill in close-range battles is noted, not to mention their dexterity and cunning, which also helps them well in battle.

The sisters undergo special training - special training of the nervous system and muscles (prana and bindu), bringing them to the limits of possible perfection and higher self-control.

Bene Gesserit adepts possess various kinds of suggestive techniques, such as, for example, Voice - the mastery of intonations and other characteristics of speech developed by special training, which allows the person who has mastered this art to control other people.

# Bene Tleilax

Bene Tleilax is a society of the Tleilaxi race, living on the planet Tleilax in the Thalim system, located on the extreme periphery of the Known Universe, or rather, in the eleventh sector of the old Empire.

## General Information

After the discovery of Tleilaxu, the Sisterhood, which saw Bene Tleilax as its competitors in mental and physical education, activated its spy system too late to discover any important information. The Tleilaxu were wise to conclude a non-interference agreement. The agreement was mutually beneficial: Tleilaxu knew about their safety, and House Corrino and the Spacing Guild were confident that they were protecting the Universe from harmful technologies while they themselves were exploiting them.

These measures were necessary since the Bene Tleilax have

always viewed war, poverty and religion as instruments of trade. Since most of the problems in these areas involved the exploitation of humans, the Tleilaxu technology placed particular emphasis on genetic production and neuropsychiatric specialists. They made thinking human tools. Face dancers, ghola, distorted mentats, Guild Navigators are examples of their products.

Throughout their existence as part of the Empire, from their discovery to the fall of the God-Emperor Leto Atreides II and the heyday of the Siona-Duncan alliance, Bene Tleilax have been objects of almost universal disgust, fear and distrust. Even in the days of fiercely competitive business and politics in the era of Corrino and Atreides, they were rejected and were the cause of resentment because of their excessive prudence.

The Tleilaxu supplied Great and Small Houses with technological needs and weapons for a bribe. But an integral part of these transactions was the sense of guilt that buyers felt for defaming the precepts of the Butlerian Jihad. The fact that the offensive nickname "Dirty Tleilaxu" was often used clearly demonstrated how defiled people felt because of the sinful trade with representatives of Tleilax, and a whole collection of prejudices and phobias was the result of these fears. For example, Fremen tended to reject Tleilaxu metal eyes, as they believed that the owner of these eyes would be secretly enslaved by their evil creators.

# Spacing Guild

The Spacing Guild is a monopolist in interstellar transportation, which is provided by Guild Navigators and banking operations.

## Description

This is an organization consisting of people who developed special skills during the Butlerian Jihad to replace and surpass machine technologies. Therefore, it is vital for the Spacing Guild to maintain the stability of Spice supplies.

Although the Spacing Guild was de jure outside of politics, the de facto position of a monopolist made it one of the pillars of the Empire. Without the guild, the Empire would have been doomed since it became impossible for communication between the worlds scattered throughout the universe and for the transfer of sardaukars to establish Imperial order.

Because of this, the Padishah Emperor and the Houses preferred to be cautious when dealing with the Space Guild.

# Creation

It was created during the Butlerian Jihad by a former employee of Holtzman's laboratory, Norma Cenva. She subsequently became the Oracle of the Guild.

# Spice

Guild Navigators (pilots) - mutants to whom the special substance melange (also known as spice) gives the ability to navigate ships through folded space without any computers. These members of the Brotherhood have both fish-like gills and lungs to facilitate breathing. The oxygen-melange mixture in the cells is quite dense, and subsequently, the pilots are engrafted with webbed feet like frogs so that they maintain their balance. Although the effectiveness of such actions is undeniable, the result is ridiculous.

## Additionally

The year of the founding of the Guild was the starting point of the Imperial chronology.

# Fish Speakers

Fish Speakers are the female division from the "Dune" universe, a series of science fiction novels by Frank Herbert. They first appear in "God Emperor of Dune."

## The Emergence

Emperor Leto Atreides II founded this organization in the period between the time of the novels "Children of Dune" and "God Emperor of Dune." For several thousand years, they were the personal guard of Emperor Leto and were under the command of ghola Duncan Idaho. They were called Fish Speakers because one of the first members of this organization spoke to fish in her visions.

## Goals

Leto II founded this order to enhance his dominion over the known universe. He felt that the existing Freman and Sardaukar organizations were not suitable for his needs. The male army, in his opinion, self-degrades in peacetime, transferring normal cruelty directed at the enemy to civilians. This leads to robbery, violence, murder and pushes people to resistance and then to political anarchy, restrained only by the presence of troops (as, for example, in the Roman Empire, when the absence of serious external enemies led to a militaristic policy, which, in turn, caused the decline of the empire).

Women, on the other hand, play the role of wives and mothers in society, raising and educating their children. Thus, after the end of the war, having returned to their natural role, they will not carry out such negative actions as male warriors. Because of this, Fish Speakers were formed exclusively from women of Fremen and Sardaukar blood. Leto trained them as fanatical, disciplined and super-efficient soldiers and police. They also developed a religious cult of worship of the emperor, which was necessary to maintain the so-called "Leto World" and advance along the Golden Path. In addition to their military role, the Fish Speakers were imperial officials. Finally, Leto used the most agile and strong Fish Speakers in its breeding program.

## Disappearance

After Leto died, Duncan Idaho and Siona Atreides took control of Fish Speakers. During the time described in the book "Heretics of Dune," their influence began to fade compared to Bene Tleilax, Ixians and Bene Gesserit. Some of the Fish Speakers went into dispersion; in the "Chapterhouse: Dune," they were considered one of the ancestors of the Honored Matres — a women's community formed during the troubles that followed the death of the God-Emperor.

# Qizarate

Qizarate is a religious and political organization dedicated to spreading the teachings of Muad'Dib throughout the Empire.

# Description

Qizarate Muad'Dib was created after the victory of Paul Muad'Dib and the Fremen at the Battle of Arrakeen in the wake of the Fremen's religious veneration of their leader. Over time, Qizarate has grown into a huge bureaucratic machine. In Arrakis, the central Qizarate building was built next to the Muad'Dib Citadel.

After Paul Atreides declared himself the new emperor, Qizarate fanned the flames of religious war throughout the universe. Jihad Muad'Dib lasted twelve years, after which Muad'Dib fanatics subdued almost all of humanity on many planets of the Empire.

By the time the jihad ended, Korba, a former fedaykin who had turned from a warrior to a priest after defeating the Harkonnens, was at the head of Qizarate. To consolidate his power, Korba took part in a conspiracy against the emperor, organized by a number of his political opponents, intending to make a martyr out of him in the event of Muad'Dib's death and lay the blame for what happened to his concubine Chani Kynes. But after an attempt on Paul Atreides, in which he lost his sight, the plot was discovered, and Korba was killed after interrogation.

After leaving for the desert, Paul Atreides began to appear in Arrakeen under the name of Preacher. In his sermons, he denounced the Qizarate priests, who adapted the teachings of Muad'Dib for their own benefit.

# Smugglers

A smuggler is a person who was engaged in illegal from the point of view of the legislation sale or transportation of goods (contraband).

## History

During the reign of the Padishah Emperor Shaddam Corrino IV, there was an influential organization of smugglers on the planet Arrakis. The significance of the Arrakis smugglers was evidenced by the fact that the Padishah Emperor himself was interested in their operations and negotiated with the smugglers through his personal friend, Count Hasimir Fenring. Duke Leto Atreides also understood their importance, and after arriving on Arrakis, he sent Gurney Halleck as an ambassador to the smugglers, offering to turn a blind eye to their operations in exchange for the duke's tithe. After the fall of the House of Atreides, Halleck became a smuggler himself until he met the survivor of the attack, Paul Atreides. In the future, Halleck maintained good relations with Arrakis smugglers.

During the Arrakis Revolt, some of the smugglers joined the rebels, and after the victory of Muad'Dib, they received posts in his empire.

The main contraband with Arrakis was Spice. The smugglers had close contacts with the Fremen: they bought Spice from the Fremen sietch and transported it in caravans to their frigates, who illegally delivered it to the Space Guild heighliner.

# LIST OF DUNE PLANETS

Here is a list of some of the 'millions of worlds' described in the Dune novels.

However, we must clarify that none of the planets that humankind explored or lived in experienced 'alien civilizations. Instead, the real advanced beings in the universe were natural humans, automatons created by humans or genetically-modified humans.

## *Arrakis*

Arrakis is a desert key planet in the Dune universe created by American writer Frank Herbert.

The entire surface of the red-orange planet, like Mars, is covered with endless deserts; sometimes, there are mountain ranges cut by numerous caves. Ice caps are located at the poles of the Dune, which indicate the presence of water on the planet in the past, and, therefore, rich vegetation and wildlife. The Arrakis sky is silver in color.

## Nature

Vegetation on the planet is very sparse and is represented mainly by small shrubs that can survive in the desert. The fauna is much more diverse, although most of it was introduced to the Dune as part of the Pardot Kynes environmental program. Among the inhabitants of the plane,t you can find desert foxes, Fennec, mice, hares, turtles, eagles, dwarf owls and arachnids with scorpions. But the main and indigenous inhabitant of Arrakis was and still is Shai-Hulud — a sandworm, a source of oxygen and a producer of Spice.

## Climate

There are frequent storms on Arrakis. Usually, the hurricane front is at least six to seven thousand kilometers wide. They are fueled by everything that adds power to them: Coriolis forces, other storms, and anything that has a little energy in it. They pick up speed to seven hundred kilometers per hour, taking with them everything that turns up: dust, sand, and so on. They rip the meat off the bones and even split the bones.

## Map

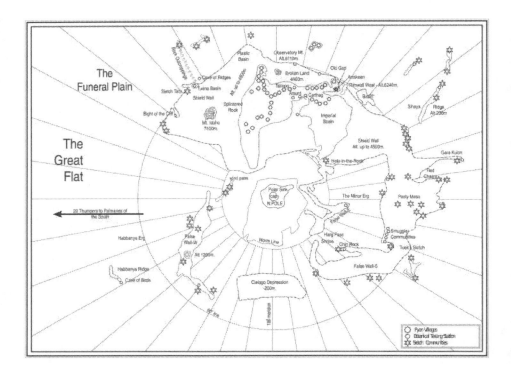

# Giedi Prime

A fictional industrial planet in the Dune universe, the metropolis of the sinister house Harkonnen, the antagonists of the Dune universe.

Human trafficking and slavery are legalized on the planet, and violent Gladiator fights are frequent entertainment among the local population.

# Ix

The ninth planet of the alpha Eridani system, known before the Butlerian Jihad as KOMOS. The name is derived from the planet's ordinal number in the Roman numbering system (IX).

Before the great Jihad, the planet KOMOS was a province of its neighbor, the planet Richez, which appointed a planetary administrator or "Exarch" to rule on behalf of the home planet's government. After the Butlerian Jihad, X became a secret source of high technology.

# Kaitain

Metropolis of the Corrino house. The planet Kaitain was chosen as the new capital of the Empire after Salusa Secundus, the former capital, became virtually uninhabitable as a result of the atomic war. Kaitain remained the capital of the Empire for a long time before Muad'Dib moved the capital to Arrakis.

The planet kaitain has large rings and four moons. Kaitain's climate is consistently temperate.

# Caladan

Metropolis of the house of Atreides. Caladan is the third planet of the Peacock Delta. Members of the House of Atreides have lived on Caladan for twenty-six generations in the ancient castle of Caladan, which was the home of Paul Atreides for his first fifteen years of life.

The surface of the green-blue planet is mostly covered with water, and the planetary climate is determined by heavy precipitation and strong winds. The surface of the planet is covered with forests, swamps, and fields.

Caladan has a strong defensive armed force with a predominance of naval and air forces. The elite Atreides troops can compete with the Emperor's Sardaukar for their fighting prowess and bravery.

# Richese

Richese is the fourth planet of the alpha Eridani system: the Equatorial diameter is 55,000 kilometers; 60 % land, 5 % freshwater lakes, 35 % salt oceans. Moderate size of polar ice caps, average annual temperature - 18 degrees, average January temperature - 2 degrees, average July temperature - 29 degrees. The planet is rich in minerals and metallic ores.

The planet is also the only source of gallanium in the seventeen sectors, a substance used in microminiaturization. The planet is the production center of Ix.

Capital of the planet Richez: Lugdunum. Population: 2 billion.

# Salusa Secundus

The third planet of the Pisces gamma system. The homeworld of House Corrino, from which the eighty-one padishah-emperors descended. It was the capital of the Empire, but after the Butlerian Jihad, the planet was burned out by the atomic war. It was later turned by the Padishah Emperor into the prison planet of the Corrino emperors and later became the basis for training his elite Sardaukar troops.

# Tleilax

The only planet of the star Talim. The Tleilaxu is a source of immoral but tolerant technological products that meet the requirements of the Butlerian Jihad. Not only did the Tleilaxu trade in simple machines, but they also produced artificial humans genetically adapted for certain purposes.

Tleilaxu - a fictional race in the Dune universe by Frank Herbert. They mostly live on their home planet, "Tleilax."

Fanatically devoted to their faith. All outsiders are called "powindah, "which roughly means" infidels." The Tleilaxu are specialists in genetics and genetic engineering. They regard the genome as the language of God.

# *Tupile*

Tupile was a region whose details were kept away from people. Although this region of the universe was somehow regarded as a single planet (AKA the "sanctuary planet"), the truth is that it was a group of several planets. Nobody except the Spacing Guild knew the actual location of Tupile, and the secret was kept away from other groups and organizations.

In the advent of the Faufreluches under House Corrino, Tupile was mainly reserved for traitors or defeated Great Houses of the Imperium for sanctuary whenever they were exiled. This punishment was meted on these categories of people if the said House disobeyed the Emperor or was defeated by a rival Great House in a War of Assassins or occurred as an act of Kanly.

Although the motive for using Tupile was unchanged during the reign of the Atreides Empire, during and after the reign of Atreides ll, there is some proof leading to the conclusion that some houses, including the remnants of the House of Harkonnen, were not exiled to Tupile. Hence, the period lost some of its stigma and mystique.

# Buzzell

Buzzell is a very cold planet, mainly surrounded by the ocean with "hardscrabble islands, none broader than a large no-ship." This planet consists of soostones, precious iridescent ornaments created by the eroded cocoons of monoped sea creatures known as Cholisters, just like pearls.

Also referred to as "punishment planet" used by the Bene Gesserit, Buzzell is ultimately the abode of the new species of aquatic sandworms.

# Corrin

In Dune, it can be observed that the Atreides-Harkonnen dispute had started millennia before "an Atreides had a Harkonnen banished for cowardice after the Battle of Corrin." Happening "near Sigma Draconis in the year 88 B.G," this war "settled the ascendancy of the ruling House from Salusa Secundus," who then adopted the name House Corrino.

Brian Herbert and Kevin J. Anderson's Legends of Dune prequel trilogy examines the incidents of the Butlerian Jihad, the launch of the human crusade against thinking machines, which snowballed into the Battle of Corrin. During the period in question, Corrin is the most crucial and significant of the Synchronized Worlds, as it was the homeworld of machine leader Ominus.

To mark mankind's total victory over the thinking machines on Corrin, Viceroy Faykan Butler adopted the name "Corrino" to establish the House that would rule humanity for more than 10,000 years.

# Ginaz

Ginaz was a planet that became popular mainly because of its Swordmasters. This planet was also the ancestral home of House Ginaz, whose reign was cut short by House Moritani in the War of Assassins.

It was identical to Old Earth in terms of size and atmosphere. While its surface consisted of over 90% of water, the land area contained dispersed sandy archipelagos with little vegetation.

## History

In the past, the world had been inhabited by a small but vicious set of warrior humans. These ancient beings greatly contributed to the war that struck during the Butlerian Jihad. They were hired as mercenaries to fight a fierce battle against the thinking machines.

The year 164 BG witnessed Hecate's asteroid fall on the planet, resulting in a huge tsunami that destroyed the major parts of the colonized islands. However, after seven decades, the civilization was restored.

After a long period of time, these people eventually evolved into the famous Swordmasters.

# Hagal

Hagal (aka the "Jewel Planet"), ruled by a County General, was regarded as the second planet of the Theta Shaowei start system. Widely known for its soostones and fire opals, Hagal was the planet where most of the rare crown treasures of the Known Universe were first found.

This planet was mined out fully during the reign of Padishah Emperor Shaddam I. Successive emperors used to sit on a throne made out of one part transparent blue-green Hagal quartz. This planet was also home to House Hagal.

# Ishia

Ishia is the second planet of Beta Tygri, a Corrino holding that had been abandoned since it was discovered.

Ishia was arid, hot, and oppressing to its life form as opposed to Rossak, a cold environment. Crops could barely survive in Ishia, except the land got a sufficient amount of energy and time for irrigation. The system required constant vigilance, as a day's lack of necessary supply could kill a field. The Wandering Zensunni referred to this planet as Albudeite (scarce water).

# Lampadas

Lampadas was the location of a Bene Gesserit Keep and also the location of their major educational and library facilities. This planet, along with many other planets, was attacked by the Honored Matres while they were returning from the Scattering to the Old Empire. During the brutal attack, out of the 7,622,014 Reverend Mothers posted to Lampadas, only Lucilla escaped the planet alive, while the sad memory of her fellow Reverend Mothers kept lingering in her mind. The efforts of the Bashar Burzmali to prevent the disaster proved abortive.

As soon as the Butlerian Jihad came to an end, Gilbertus Albans allocated a remote marshlanatttea of Lampadas as the original location of the Mentat School.

# *Synchrony*

The Thinking Machine Empire was rebuilt after its defeat at the Battle of Corrin. Thereafter, Synchrony became the planet capital. Synchrony planet came into being after a series of flowmetal and free-moving machines gathered into various shapes and buildings as instructed by the Evermind.

# THE MOST COMMON ANIMALS IN THE DUNE

## *Kangaroo mouse*

The kangaroo mouse or muad'dib is an animal that has adapted to the conditions of Arrakis, resembling a jerboa.

The Fremen admire the muad'dib because of the animal's ability to survive in the desert: he creates water for himself, hides from the daytime sun, and comes out on a cool night, he is fertile. The Fremen believed that the Muad'dib knew the wisdom of the Desert.

After the Fremen adopted Paul Atreides into their tribe, he chose the name Paul Muad'Dib as the male name worn openly. However, the Fremen often abbreviated this name, calling their leader simply Muad'Dib.

## *Kulon*

Kulon is a desert donkey, one of the few domestic animals in Arrakis.

Kulons originate from the Asian steppes of Terra. Some of the smugglers in Arrakis used domesticated kulons as beasts of burden, but the water consumption was too high, even with specially modified still suits.

# Laza tiger

Laza tigers - are large cats. They were first imported to the planet Salusa Secundus. These beasts were most often used in gladiatorial battles for many centuries.

Genetic manipulations have erased some of the features inherent in ancestral terrestrial forms but provided cats with new ones. The animals still have long fangs. The muzzle is broad, and the eyes are large and intelligent. Large paws that provide good support on uneven rocky ground, claws more than ten centimeters long are hidden, and the pressure of the skin folds constantly sharpens them so that the ends of the claws are razor sharp. The coat is smooth, slightly brownish - a protective color in the desert Sands.

Before the tigers grow up, the kittens are implanted in the brain with a control device that makes them obedient to the will of anyone who has the appropriate transmitter.

# Sandtrout

Sandtrout - the larval form of the sandworm, half-plants, and half-animals that inhabit the deep sand layers on the planet Arrakis. Outwardly described as large freshwater leeches, amorphous clots, or slugs.

Sandtrout are found in large numbers in the Sands of Arrakis, playing a crucial role in its ecosystem. It is the trout that turned the surface of the planet into a desert, encapsulating large bodies of water and allowing adult sandworms to survive since they could not live in wet soil.

Many of the trout died during the natural life cycle of the planet; those that survived eventually grew over thousands of years into giant sandworms that plowed the Sands of Arrakis.

## History

For many hundreds of years before the arrival of the Atreides on Arrakis, sandtrout have been brought there from some other planet. On Arrakis, trout began to multiply to such an extent that they destroyed the former ecosystem of this once-wet planet. By encapsulating all the water, the sandtrout was able to turn into a sandworm. Only the salt basins lost in the desert remained of the former huge seas.

# *Sandworm*

The Sandworm or Shai Hulud is an animal of Arrakis, also known as the Creator, or Great-Grandfather of the Desert, the Old Man of the Desert, and Father of Eternity. Pronounced in a special tone or written in capital letters means the deity of the earth - a terrifying underground demon from the beliefs of the Fremen.

## Description

The sandworm grows to a huge size (individual specimens in the deep desert exceed 400 meters in length) and lives for quite a long time if it is not killed by one of its fellows, or if the worm does not die, being poisoned by water, which is poisonous for them.

## Stages Of Shai-Hulud

During their development, worms go through several stages. The embryonic stage is called sandtrout and is a shapeless, single-celled, semi-plant and semi-animal creature that inhabits deep sandy layers.

A worm is formed when large numbers of sandtrout combine into a single organism. If the worm is exposed to water, it breaks up into a lot of sandtrout, which can later be combined again into a worm, so there is a closed cycle of sandworms and trout.

## Role In The Ecosystem Of Arrakis

Sandworms inhabit almost all the sandy areas of Arrakis and play an important role in ecology. Melange on Arrakis is mainly the result of the life of sandworms, which is why they are also called Spice givers; besides, the worms emit oxygen. From the teeth of the dead Shai-Hulud, the Fremen make their semi-ritual weapons, the Krisknife, and by drowning a small worm, they get the Water of Life. Adult worms are used by Fremen as vehicles.

## Riders Of Shai-Hulud

A person who can jump on a sandworm and control it, the Fremen call the Desert Rider, or simply the Rider. To climb onto the "back" of the worm, the Fremen use large hooks on a long, folding handle. The worm is controlled by these same hooks. The Fremen who first prepares to jump on the worm usually acts as the helmsman.

# A CATALOG OF DUNE TERMINOLOGY

Ted West

## A

**Aba** - free outfit of Fremen women, more often black.

**Adab** - an important memory that comes to a person against his will.

**Axlotl tank** - ghola growing technology. In fact, these are women from the Bene Tleilaxu Order without the spinal cord and brain, used as incubators.

**Alam al-Mithal** - a mystical world of parables where there are no physical restrictions.

**Ampoliros** - the flying Dutchman of space legends, a free-drifting starship without a crew or with a dead crew.

**Assassins** - specialists in the killing, usually in the service of the ruling houses.

**Aumas** - a poison that is added only in solid food.

**Anti-fatigue Pills** – a powerful stimulant utilized by the military.

**Arcana** – the covert doctrines of the Bene Gesserit.

**Armored Screen** – a security apparatus designed in the form of a large protective shield.

**Arrakeen** – the foremost settlement on Arrakis; the base of the planetary administration for many years.

**Assyria** – an antique kingdom on ancient earth. It was home to the adversaries of the forebears of the Bene Gesserit.

**Auliya** – according to the beliefs of the Zensunni Wanderers, this refers to God's handmaiden or the woman at the right hand of God.

# B

**Bashar** - a military rank above the level of colonel, usually the rank of commander of the military forces of the planet, as well as among the sardaukars.

**Bindu** - a word applied to the nervous system, primarily to train it.

**Burseg** - a Sardaukar battle General.

**Bedwine** – a roving desert-dweller; this often applied to the Ichwan Bedwine, the league of all Fremen on Arrakis.

**Behemoth** – this is a demon or a huge sandworm, according to Fremen beliefs. Alternatively, this may also apply to an ancient type of ship or sea monster.

**Berserker** – this refers to death fighters of the fishspeakers. It was the norm for individuals who have committed a crime to be punished with an order to carry out a Berserker or suicide mission.

# C

**Cymek** - a machine controlled by the human brain; that is, in the aggregate, it is a cyborg.

**Chakobsa** - the language of the Fremen, the so-called "magnetic language," derived in part from the fictional ancient language of Bhotani (or Bhotani Jib). It is a mixture of several adverbs, distorted for the sake of secrecy.

**Coriolis Storm** – this is a sandstorm on Arrakis. They occur when the wind coming across the open flatlands is magnified by the revolutionary movement of the planet up to a speed of 700 kilometers per hour.

**Caseri** – a title given to a ruler. It may have emanated during the days of the ancient empire.

# D

**Distrans** - a device that removes the "imprint" of the central nervous system of a living being.

**Defensive shield** - a protective shield is a protective force field created by a Holtzmann generator.

**Deathstill** – an apparatus used by the Fremen to remove every bit of moisture from a living or dead human/creature.

**Dune Men** – an informal term that describes men who toiled to gather the spice melange amongst the sand dunes located on Planet Arrakis. It could also refer to the sand workers and spice hunters.

**Dust Chasm** – these are deep cracks or depressions on the desert of Arrakis, which is currently filled with dust. It can also refer to a weather event.

# E

**Ellaca Drug** – this is a narcotic created through the burning of the blood-grained elacca wood gotten from Ecaz. This drug takes away the human desire for self-preservation; it is often applied to slave gladiators to prepare them for the ring.

**Erg** – a wide and horizontal desert area filled with wind-swept sand with sparse or zero vegetative cover.

# F

**Face Dancers** – these are creatures created by Tleilaxu. They have the ability to perfectly imitate humans and go unnoticed, even after the application of all known means of detection.

**Face Flaps** – this forms part of the face mask of a still suit and keeps the wearer safe from fine dust.

**Favrashi** – this term was introduced by Leto II as a description of the soul, collective subconscious, source of archetypes, and the storehouse of all pain and happiness.

**Fedaykin** – Death fighters of Fremen, personally trained by Paul Atreides. According to ancient lore, they are a group formed to right a wrong. Members pledge their lives to this purpose.

# G

**Guild Navigator** - creatures in the service of the Space Guild, previously humans, but mutated under the influence of the spice and now dependent on it; only guild navigators are capable of plotting optimal travel routes in space.

**The Grand Convention** - the highest legislative Pact of the Empire, regulating relations between the Emperor, the Landsraad, and the space Guild, which has a monopoly on interplanetary transportation.

**Gom Jabbar** - "the enemy of arrogance" is a special needle, at the tip of which was the poison metacyanide. Used by the Bene Gesserit to test people.

# H

**Highliner** - the largest spacecraft used for interstellar travel. The main freighter in the Space Guild's transportation system.

**Harvester, Harvester Factory, Crawler** - Spice extraction machine.

**Holtzman Effect** - a scientific phenomenon in the Dune universe.

**Habbanya** – a region located in the Northern hemisphere of Arrakis. It is made up of a mountain ridge and part of the Erg.

**House Ferrets** – these are small, watchful animals kept by all the planetary houses to warn them of intruders. They can also keep harmful vermin, particularly 'infectious agents' at bay.

# I

**Inkvine** – creeping plant found on Giedi Prime, often used as a whip in the slave pens of Giedi. Victims were scarred by beet-colored tattoos that resulted in lingering pains that lasted for several years.

**Ixian Core** – the base of the technological association led by Ix.

**Ixian Probe** – an apparatus that captures the sentiments of a living or dead individual for inspection. The device can be impeded by the substance shere.

# J

**Jadacha** – A Jadacha-hermaphrodit as the Face Dancers refers to an individual possessing no physical or mental sexual orientation but may choose to alter its physical appearance to mimic another individual of any sex or danger.

**Jalalud-Din** – this is a settlement on Arrakis located close to the great gap in the shield wall.

**Jihad** – the absolute purpose or struggle. It often applies to the Butlerian Jihad or Fremen Holy War.

**Jihad, Butlerian** – this is the great rebellion against thinking machines and machine culture.

# K

**Kwisatz Haderach** - this is what the bene Gesserit sisters called the goal of their breeding program: a man who can look into the genetic memory of his ancestors, both female and male, inaccessible to the sisters, lines.

**Kizara Tafwid** - Fremen clergymen of the Muad'Dib religion.

**Kanly** – a formal dispute or vendetta existing within the statutes of the great convention carried out in line with the most stringent regulations. Initially, the regulations were put in place to ensure the safety of innocent spectators.

**Krimskell Rope** – this is a rope created from Krimskell fiber. It is usually utilized by Troopers for effective crowd-control and to apprehend possible outlaws.

# L

**Lasgun, Lasegun** - a continuous (non-pulsed) laser. Its use as a weapon is limited by the widespread use of force fields, since a subatomic explosion occurs when the beam comes into contact with it.

**Life Scanner** – these are Ixian machines used to detect life signals on a planet or a particular area. The rays from the scanners can be thwarted by particular algae, which were utilized as live protection shields.

# M

**Melange** - See the description of the term Spice.

**Mentat** - a human "computer" with outstanding analytical and computational abilities.

# N

**Na-Baron** - the title of the official successor to the Baron. The prefix "Na-" means the next in line.

**No-chamber** - a structure that can hide everything inside and itself from foresight.

**Nezhoni Scarf** - this is a scarf-pad worn by married Fremen women, who have birthed a male child, or those who are romantically involved. The Nezhoni scarf is worn on the forehead underneath a stillsuit.

**Nullentropy** – this is a technology that helps to halt the natural cycles of time like decomposition. It aided the preservation of such matter as human cells over millennia without any harm coming to them.

# O

**Ornithopter, in common parlance, a thopter** - an aircraft that creates lift by flapping its wings.

**Obliterators** – these are acclaimed Matre weapons of mass destruction. They work by combusting the atmosphere of a planet and afterward, the planet's surface.

# P

**Padishah Emperor** - the title of the ruler of the Empire.

**Prana** - the designation of the body's muscle groups when teaching higher self-control.

# R

**Reverend Mother** - the title of a Bene Gesserit woman who has successfully completed training.

**Razzia** - semi-pirate raid.

# S

**Sandtrout** - young sandworms. The Fremen called them Little Makers.

**Sandworm** - a giant animal of the planet Arrakis that existed only on it until the era of Emperor Leto II.

**Spice, also Melange** - a mind-expanding substance. It is a product of a sandworm's activity. It is used to replace prohibited intelligent machines (robots and computers) with specially trained people, for example, navigators must calculate interstellar flights, are also needed by Mentans.

**Solar** - the main currency of the Empire. Its purchasing power is determined by meetings held every 400 years between the Guild, Landsraad, and the Emperor.

# W

**Water of Life** – this is a Roxi fluid exhaled by a drowning sandworm. It is utilized by Fremen Reverend Mothers in the spice of agony.

**Wind Trap** – this is an apparatus used on Arrakis to capture moisture from the air. It is often hidden on the warren rock.

# Z

**Zaha** – Morning nap on Arrakis.

**Zanadig** – An expletive used by the Fremen.

# THINGS YOU SHOULD KNOW ABOUT SPICE MELANGE

The Spice Melange, also known simply as 'the spice,' is an awareness spectrum narcotic created through natural processes. It became a cornerstone of commerce and technological development in the known universe for millennia.

Besides the aforementioned importance of the spice mélange, the substance was vital to voyages and cultural development since it played a paramount role in ensuring the success of space travel. It helps navigators to guide space ships safely through warp space.

It was discovered many years before House Atreides shot into prominence and through that time, it was solely produced on the planet Arrakis. The exclusivity of production was necessitated because the conditions necessary for creating the melange were specific to the planet Arrakis and could be found nowhere else. The Bene Tleilax successfully reproduced the conditions alluded to above some 1500 years after the demise of the God-Emperor Leto II.

## *Origin*

The spice emanated from the planet Arrakis, where its production took place in the depths of the sands. The process of its creation involves a mixture of fungal excretions of sandtrout and water to form a pre-spice mass.

This spice mass is then brought to the desert surface by an explosion of pressure. Afterward, a melange will form from the mass exposed to the intense heat and air of the planet. At the end of a worm's life span, sandtrouts are expelled into the sand and the process of creation begins anew.

# Future Importance

At the point when House Atreides found themselves on Arrakis, melange had grown into the sole resource able to make or break the empire. The melange's prominence moved Arrakis from a distant, impoverished, and insignificant desert world to a highly valued fiefdom. Taking charge of the spice managing operations were considered prestigious but hectic.

Assembling the spice was impeded by the hostile and territorial sandworms and also by the guerrilla schemes the Fremen applied because they hated the presence of the off-worlders (particular imperial representatives) who collected the spice for their personal use.

# THEMES AND IDEAS IN THE DUNE NOVELS

In the Dune novels, Frank Herbert explored several concepts revolving around philosophy, religion, psychology, politics, and ecology. However, underneath his Dune story is the question of human survival and evolution.

Frank has a huge fan base who have become fanatics of his work, both fiction and nonfiction. As a result, he has become like an authority on the subject matter he explored in his books.

**Let's dive into the key themes Herbert explored in his work. They are:**

1.  **Leadership**: In his Dune novels, he dwelt on the tendency of human beings to blindly depend and follow leaders who are charismatic. He also explored the pros and cons of government and bureaucracy.

2.  **Ecology**: Among many other science fiction writers, Herbert was part of the first set of science fiction writers with some ideas on systemic thinking and popular ecology. He gave lots of reasons for the necessity for humans to engage in more systemic thinking and also think long-term.

3.  He exposes how politics, religion, and power are closely related.

4.  **The survival and evolution of human beings:** In the novels, the Fremen, the Sardaukar, and the Dosadi are

subjected to the harsh environment and living conditions. As a result, it turned them into the most dangerous, ruthless, and superior races in the novel.

5. **Human prospects and potential**: Herbert proposed Mentats, the Bene Tleilax, and the Bene Gesserit as different visions of human potential.

6. **Sanity and madness**: These two opposites were explored in the Dune novels. As a fan of the works of Thomas Szasz and the anti-psychiatry movement, Frank Herbert often posed the question, "What is sane?" Through some characters, like Piter De Vries, which Herbert used to showcase insane behaviors and psychopathies, Herbert suggests that regular and unusual are relative that humans are sometimes inexperienced to relate to one another, specifically on the idea of statistical regularity.

7. How consciousness-altering chemicals affect Human beings and their consequences. This is seen in the depiction of the effects and consequences of the spice in Dune Saga, the "Jaspers" fungus in The Santaroga Barrier, and the Kelp in the Destination: Void sequence.

8. **Sociobiology**: The relationship between our instincts, behavior, and society. Basically, it borders on the role our instincts play in influencing how we behave and our society.

9. He also exposes the concepts of learning, teaching, and thinking.

10. Frank Herbert offered a more precise perspective on these ideas rather than a formulaic approach to providing his answers.

# More:

# Prophecy and Foresight

The Atreides family, and Paul in particular, capitalize on coincidences that make it appear as though Paul is destined to be a key leader and savior. This is what causes the Bene Gesserit to not assassinate his mother for the "crime" of not following their breeding program, and later it influences the decision of the Fremen to follow Paul on what they believe to be a holy war. Paul is eventually regarded as a messiah of sorts, however such foresight and special skills that he possesses come chiefly from his training and his use of the spice drug. Eventually, the text reveals that Paul is not truly all-knowing or all-powerful. Ultimately, he loses some of his power and, blind, retreats into the desert.

One of the psychic gifts Paul has, due to his use of the spice trance, is limited knowledge of the future. Among the visions he has is the eventual decline and extinction of humankind. One of the reasons he seeks power is to try to prevent that. Many of the things Paul predict come to pass because of actions he deliberately takes and events he personally sets into motion. Paul's foresight is not infinite, nor is it completely reliable. He does not predict the birth of his twin children, and Leto comes as a total surprise. He also does not predict the explosion that blinds him physically, forcing him to rely on his foresight as a substitute for his actual eyes. Yet this precognition too eventually fails him.

# Family Loyalty

"House" Atreides is a noble family sent by the Emperor to rule the desert planet of Dune. They are part of a somewhat feudal aristocracy. The authority of each House depends on the favor of the Emperor. But loyalty to one's House, or to the House an individual serves in the case of Duncan Idaho, is based on more than genetics.

The ability of the Bene Gesserit to recall the memories of their ancestors, and the fact they have the ability to mesmerize and subvert powerful men into marrying them, thereby becoming the de facto power behind the throne, is a plot device that ensures most people are aware of who their parents are. The Fremen are organized into clan-like nomadic tribes based chiefly on family ties.

# Holy War

Paul uses the Fremen and the Bene Gesserit to seize control of the spice melange trade, which is critical to interstellar travel.

The Bene Gesserit and the Fremen both believe him to be a messiah who has divine power, and they follow him because they believe their religion tells them to do so. Yet Paul's aspirations reach far beyond the planet of Arrakis.

# Memory

Through their use of the spice drug, the Bene Gesserit (like Paul) are able to access the memories and actual personalities of their ancestors, allowing an ancestor to briefly take over their bodies. One of the reasons Paul's sister Alia is considered an Abomination, having been exposed to the spice trance prior to birth, is because she never has an opportunity to fully develop her own personality, will, or character and is in constant danger of being overwhelmed by an ancestor's personality.

So although Alia has preternatural knowledge and intelligence even as a child, the Bene Gesserit regard her as mistrust due to her "disease" of Abomination, which they believe can be cured only by death.

# Rebirth and Resurrection

Paul uses the Fremen and the Bene Gesserit to seize control of the spice melange trade, which is critical to interstellar travel.

The Bene Gesserit and the Fremen both believe him to be a messiah who has divine power, and they follow him because they believe their religion tells them to do so. Yet Paul's aspirations reach far beyond the planet of Arrakis.

# INTERESTING FACTS ABOUT "DUNE" AND THE DUNIVERSE

## 1. Water

Among the Fremen, water is scarce. Even the water in their bodies, necessary for their survival, is considered to not be owned by the person whose body it is, but by the whole clan. Giving, sharing, or exchanging water with another person carries with it a family-like obligation. Likewise, the Fremen believe that they do not own their own lives, and that they exist solely to advance a higher purpose.

2. In the novel, the ecology of the planet Arrakis is thought out in great detail. This was done at a time when there was no such word yet. Sandworms are the backbone of the ecosystem: they produce spice and oxygen, themselves an organosilicon form of life and, in fact, represent living thermonuclear reactors. Water is deadly for them.

## 3. Desert

Arrakis, or Dune as the locals call it, is a desert planet. It has no large bodies of surface water. Aside from small human settlements and a few larger cities, much of the planet is the home of the sandworms. These worms are the key to Melange or spice production, and therefore to the galactic economy. However the desert environment makes for a very primitive standard of living throughout most of the planet, and all of Fremen society is centered around desert survival.

4. Fictional place names from Herbert's novel are now used by astronomers to name objects on the surface of Titan. This tradition began in 2009, when one of the plains of the largest satellite of Saturn was named after the fictional planet Chusuk.

## 5. Technology

Part of the struggle in the novel comes from the fact that modern technology can't always work on Dune. The sandworms, which are attracted to electromagnetic fields and to anything that makes a rhythmic noise, prowl the desert and are capable of devouring an ornithopter and everyone inside. Such technology as the Fremen have typically rely on things besides metal and electricity.

6. The humanity that inhabits the world of Dune has absorbed the features of many cultures and is replete with a lot of differ-

ent references. You will probably hear a lot of Arabic in Arrakian terminology. There are a lot of Arabic and middle Eastern words in Herbert's books. Moreover, both direct borrowings and linguistic constructions are based on motives. Al-Sayal, Hajj, Jihad, Shaitan, Burhan, Fedaykin... hundreds and hundreds of terms. But at the same time, much is taken from other languages. There are Slavic names - for example, Vladimir. Many Buddhist and near - Buddhist terms-Zen Buddhism, prana, bindu. Central American Tleilaxu and axolotl, Greek Atreides.

## 7. Crysknife

A crysknife is a rare weapon made from the tooth of a sandworm. When "keyed" to a particular person, it can only be used by that person. Since it is not metal, it has certain technical advantages in terms of overcoming electromagnetic shields. A uniquely Fremen weapon, the crysknife has religious symbolism due to its association with the sandworms. Paul's mother refers to the crysknife as a "maker" while stumbling for an appropriate word, although in reality it is also a destroyer.

# LEGACY

Undoubtedly, Dune has influenced and brought about several other art pieces from novels to games, music, movies, comic books, etc. Today, it has received the title of the most powerful and relevant science fiction novels of all time.

Star Wars is an example of a science fiction work inspired by Dune. In pop culture, Dune was referenced in works like Star Trek, the Kingkiller Chronicle, and Futurama. Precisely, the Hayao Miyazaki's anime film Nausicaä of the Valley of the Wind (1984) cited Dune as the major inspiration.

In 2013, the New Yorker's Jon Michaud stated, "What's curious about Dune's stature is that it has not penetrated popular culture in the way that The Lord of the Rings and Star Wars have." Jon further applauded Herbert's "clever authorial decision" to exclude robots and computers, which are seeming essentials in science fiction, from his fictional universe. However, Jon suggests that this exclusion of robots and computers might be the reason why Dune doesn't have "true fandom among science-fiction fans."

# DUNE UNIVERSE CANON

The Canon of the Dune Universe is a system of rules that determines the "truth" of the description of a particular phenomenon from the point of view of the Dune Universe.

Following the death of Dune Universe author Frank Herbert in February 1986, all rights to the Dune brand were transferred to Herbert Properties LLC, the official copyright holder of the writer's legacy.

## The canonicity of books by B. Herbert and K. Anderson's

Frank Herbert's son Brian, along with co-author Kevin Anderson, wrote many novels and short stories about the Dune universe that was initially a significant commercial success; the first of these was released in 1999. The authors stated that the plot of their books is mainly based on unpublished notes by Frank Herbert. The novels describe events that took place before and after the time described in the novel "Dune," for example, the Butlerian Jihad.

All events described in the books of Herbert Jr. and Andersen were published with the approval of Herbert Properties LLC and are, therefore, considered official Canon.

Before his death, Frank Herbert was working on the seventh and final novel of The Chronicles of Dune series, known under the working title Dune 7. Based on these drafts, Herbert Jr. and Anderson published two novels, Hunters of Dune (2006) and Sandworms of Dune (2007), considered to be the conclusion of the Dune saga.

Nevertheless, many readers believe that the books of Herbert Jr. and Anderson are significantly inferior to the literary data of the novels of Classic Dune by Frank Herbert, differ greatly in style and spirit, and also have a large number of inconsistencies with the works of their predecessors in factual details.

The discrepancies range from minor to the global philosophy of Frank Herbert's "Dune."

In an attempt to explain such discrepancies in the novel "Paul of Dune" (2008), the authors persistently pursued the idea that the novels of Classical Dune should be viewed as "intra-universe" documents written by Irulan Corrino and, therefore, not entirely reliable.

Also, the novel claimed that Paul Atreides deliberately hid certain aspects of his life from Irulan, especially during his childhood years. Based on this, Herbert Jr. and Anderson consider their novels more canonical than the works of the original Dune.

# The Canonicity of the Dune Encyclopedia

The Dune Encyclopedia was published in 1984. The encyclopedia has significantly expanded and concretized ideas about technical devices, celestial bodies... objects mentioned in the novels by Frank Herbert.

The authors of the encyclopedia, published under the editorship of the University of California professor Willis McNally, were professionals in various sciences such as astronomy and linguistics.

Frank Herbert approved of the publication but noted that his vision on some of the issues described in it is somewhat different.

The Dune Encyclopedia was well-received by many readers, but Herbert Properties LLC refused to recognize it as canonical.

# IS DUNE WORTH YOUR TIME?

Here are a few things the novels explored: human stellar exploration, human mental & physical evolution, ecology (the first science fiction book to do this), economics, and several future traditional science fiction tropes of stellar empires in the future. It's a two-way street, so you may or may not like it.

Dune is pretty large and widespread, and even Herbert gets lost in the story at times. In my opinion, Frank's books are amazing, and the first trilogy that he wrote remains the most loved amongst true fans of Dunes. However, while Herbert's son and Kevin further expanded the Duniverse, it is good but not exactly the best. Compared to Frank's works, they are poor, but this is just my opinion.

My suggestion? Start with the initial trilogy first. The fact that Dune is popular and has won quite a lot of awards is a great sign that it is an amazing fiction work. Honestly, it is not something you can quickly read. However, I can say that the Duniverse novels and short stories are entirely worth your time, especially if you love science fiction.

If all your love for science fiction is hinged on seeing robots, spaceships, computers, and clear good/bad characters, you still would like Dune. And if you're all about the literary and classic science fiction, then Dune will absolutely blow you away.

# Dear Readers!

Thank You for Purchasing & Reading! Hope this can help y'all to love the Dune as much as I do! Enjoy!

If you leave without writing a review about the guide, one sad author will become more... :)

**Ted West.**

Made in the USA
Las Vegas, NV
29 November 2023

81620958R00077